# STRETCH OUT YOUR HAND

## EXPLORING HEALING PRAYER

Tilda Norberg and Robert D. Webber

UPPER ROOM BOOKS®
NASHVILLE

*Stretch Out Your Hand: Exploring Healing Prayer*
Copyright © 1998 by Tilda Norberg and Robert D. Webber
All rights reserved.

*Stretch Out Your Hand* was originally published by United Church Press. This is a revised edition.

The scripture quotations contained herein are from the New Revised Standard Version Bible, copyright © 1989 by the Division of Christian Education of the National Council of Churches of Christ in the USA. Used by permission. All rights reserved.

Portions of "A Service of Social Exorcism" are taken from *Claiming All Things for God* by George D. McClain, © 1998 by Abingdon Press, and are reprinted by permission of the publisher. The main portion of the worship service is an adaptation by Tilda Norberg of a service written by George D. McClain and is used here with permission.

Cover Design: Gore Studio, Inc.
Interior Design: Charles Sutherland
Print ISBN: 978-0-8358-0872-9

*Library of Congress Cataloging-in-Publication Data*
Norberg, Tilda.
     Stretch out your hand: exploring healing prayer / Tilda Norberg and Robert D. Webber. — Rev. ed.
     p.   cm.
     Includes bibliographical references.
     ISBN 0-8358-0872-6
     1. Spiritual healing. 2. Prayer-Christianity. I. Webber, Robert D.  II. Title.
     BV227.N67  1999
     234'.131-dc21                     98-20638
                                           CIP

To Our Spouses

George D. McClain
and
Ann Atlee Webber

# CONTENTS

Preface to the Revised Edition                                          6

1.   Stretch Our Your Hand: Stories of Healing                          9

2.   Frequently Asked Questions about Healing                          28

3.   Praying for the Person God Is Calling Me to Be                    49

4.   A Simple Gift: Praying for Another's Healing                      72

5.   Social Healing: Praying for Institutions                         91

6.   The Church as a Healing Community                                114

Notes                                                                132

Selected Bibliography                                                139

# PREFACE TO THE REVISED EDITION

This book represents a complete revision and updating of a work by the same name originally published in 1990. We are grateful that the book struck a responsive chord in many people desiring to explore healing prayer and are happy that the book now will be available to a new and wider audience of spiritual explorers.

The book was born out of the authors' two separate Christian faith journeys. In the first chapter we tell how each of us came to explore healing prayer. Reluctant at first, with many questions and hesitations, we slowly became convinced that God does indeed use ordinary folks to heal. We saw that we could seldom predict how God would work in a given situation. In addition, we observed that sometimes people stood in the way of God's healing work. From these discoveries we share our understanding of Christian healing.

Healing through prayer sometimes raises almost as many questions as it answers. Why isn't everyone healed? What is the role of faith? Is it fair to offer healing prayer to a suffering person, only to have him or her suffer deep disappointment when the healing does not occur?

Before either of us began to be comfortable identifying with the healing ministry, we wrestled with these and many other questions. Yet, as we began to reflect theologically on our experience, both of us came to a greatly renewed faith in the power and love of Jesus Christ. As we moved beyond simplistic formulas, we saw how important the questions are. Chapter 1 of this book introduces Jesus' ministry of healing and situates healing prayer in the contexts of church history and of our personal experience with healing. Chapter 2 deals with some of the questions that arose for us and that, we believe, may be important for other seekers attempting to understand the value of healing prayer.

We speak personally about our experiences, based on years of engaging in healing ministry and of training pastors, laypeople, and seminarians. We draw upon this practical experience in chapters 3 and 4. There we make suggestions for persons as they pray for their own healing and for the healing of others. We also relate numerous stories of people who have been healed in various ways. (They have given permission for their stories to be told; their names and a few identifying circumstances have been changed.) We include the stories for two reasons. First, credible stories can nurture faith. And second, healing is usually experienced before it is understood. As a rule, people respond to healing with their hearts before their intellects catch up. We invite you to hear these stories from your "heart of faith."

The explosion of interest in healing in the last fifteen years is a sign that the Holy Spirit renews the church. The church, we believe, is being summoned by God to become an intentional community of healing. We see the dawn of a new spirituality—or the revival of an old one!—that unites concerns for wholeness of the body, mind, spirit, and emotions with concerns for the sociopolitical fabric in which we live. Too long has the church been divided between "spiritual" Christians and "political-activist" Christians. We believe that these ministries belong together. In chapter 5 we discuss the church's unique spiritual resources for the healing of political and institutional structures. In the last chapter, we offer a vision of the church as a healing community and suggest some ways congregations can begin to embody Jesus' healing ministry.

We hope this book will open a door for Christians to enter a new phase in their faith journey. We hope it will help them look honestly at the hard questions about healing and discover some answers that will free them to continue the journey. We hope that as Christians are emboldened to claim the ministry of personal and political healing, the church will be renewed.

Most of all, we hope this book will be a catalyst for readers to experience the healing love of Jesus firsthand—both during those times when they are in need of healing and when they are called upon to be a channel for the healing of others. Many people have told us that their personal encounters with the healing love of Jesus kindle joyful faith. It is happening for us. May this happen for you.

We thank the many people—friends, teachers, clients, students— who taught, encouraged, and challenged us along the way. We are especially grateful to George McClain, who read the manuscript and made countless valuable suggestions. We thank Ann Atlee Webber, who provided technical and moral support, and Diane Large, who cheerfully typed and retyped the manuscript. Finally, we thank those who have allowed their stories to be told, and the many others who shared with us their experiences of healing prayer.

# Stretch Out Your Hand: Stories of Healing

One day when he was visiting a synagogue, Jesus saw a man with a withered hand (Mark 3:1-6). Tension was in the air. The opponents of Jesus were waiting to see if Jesus, the popular teacher and healer, would heal the man on the Sabbath. Of course Jesus chose the way of love and compassion—the truthful, risky, passionate, dramatic way that was almost guaranteed to get him into trouble. It is unthinkable to us that he would act otherwise.

He called the man to him: "Come forward." Mark does not tell us how the man felt about being a part in this drama. Was he afraid? Self-conscious? Hopeful? Not daring to allow himself to hope at all? But something was asked of him, and he responded. He rose and moved toward Jesus. Mark does tell us how Jesus felt. He looked at the congregation "with anger; . . . grieved at their hardness of heart." "Is it lawful to do good or to do harm on the sabbath, to save life or to kill?" Imagine those words slicing through the air with great authority, cutting through custom and inertia. Imagine Jesus gazing with love at the man who stood before him. Hear the gentle yet compelling words: "Stretch out your hand." Jesus invited the man to declare himself, to act in faith on behalf of his own healing. Again the man obeyed, and his hand was restored. What an event: a withered hand was healed in front of people's eyes! Opponents and followers alike saw in concrete terms what the coming of God's rule means. Surely the man, looking with amazement at his newly restored hand, was stunned and transformed. More than a hand had been touched.

The words of Jesus echo through the centuries: "Stretch out your hand." Imagine Jesus saying that to you. Perhaps you can hear in these words an invitation to step out in faith—to let your intellect explore new pathways and allow yourself experiences that might shape your faith in a new way. Maybe you too are being asked to act in faith for your own healing.

Or perhaps you can hear Jesus inviting you to stretch out your hand in compassion to others who need healing. If you have never put your hands on another who is hurting, never prayed for healing, this may indeed be a "stretch" for you.

## *Images of Healing Ministry*

When we open the door to the exploration of healing prayer, we find a bewildering variety of theologies and styles in the practice of the healing ministry today. Most of us are familiar with healers who appear on television, who seem to work astonishing miracles right in front of the camera. We may be intrigued by them, but we may also suspect that it is the emotionalism that "cures." We may wonder what happens to people when the high wears off. Admittedly, some are healed at such services, but we may be turned off by the dramatic, simplistic style of the healer. Such a healer may loudly command cancer to go away. Crippled patients may be urged to "claim their healing" by throwing down their crutches then and there. We may wonder what in the world is going on when we observe people falling backward or crying out at the healer's touch. In contrast to this high drama, we also may be familiar with a dignified and quiet liturgical service of healing prayer. In such a service, the pastor prays the same prescribed short prayer while touching or anointing each person who is quietly kneeling at the altar rail. In this setting we might wonder if there is room for any emotion at all.

Between these two poles there is great diversity. Interest in Christian healing has grown phenomenally in the church in recent years. Healing services seem to have sprung up everywhere, reflecting wide variations of style, custom, and theology.

Beyond the Christian community, consider as well the bewildering variety of non-Christian healers who work with crystals, or colored lights, or even the "channeling" of spirits of the dead.

Those engaged in these differing healing practices seem to be involved in some form of ministry of spiritual healing. No wonder some are confused and come to an inquiry of healing with certain fears and prejudices. This was certainly true for us, the authors, as we stepped gingerly into the stream that eventually propelled us into healing ministry. We tell our stories not to provide a road map for anyone else but to introduce ourselves and to suggest that many other such stories are unfolding as the Holy Spirit prods the church to pray for healing. This, then, is what happened for us.

## Tilda's Story

While a student at Union Theological Seminary in New York City, I was employed by the East Harlem Protestant Parish to work with a teenage street gang. I was greatly moved by the needs of "my" kids and by the willingness of the parish to help them. I was also inspired by the genuine devotion and worship of this congregation. They were not only people of prayer but also of action. They lived their faith, and they were passionate about bringing healing to the social fabric of East Harlem. After graduation I felt called to serve God as a parish minister partly because this church gave me a vision of how vital a parish could be. I had not reckoned, however, with the obstacles I would encounter in 1966 as a woman trying to serve a church. Every time I explored a position in parish ministry I met with closed doors. Some of these doors slammed shut with words of ridicule and rejection. Others were shut with gentleness and concern, but still firmly shut.

Parish ministry seemed closed to me, yet how urgently I yearned for it! I physically ached to be a pastor—to nurture and love a congregation—but it seemed impossible. In the wake of constant rejection, self-doubts began to creep in. Was there, I wondered, something terribly wrong with me? Or was the church so hopelessly sexist that a woman pastor was unthinkable? Had I misunderstood God's call all along? Maybe going to seminary was just a costly mistake. I became depressed and angry.

About this time I began training as a psychotherapist, because it seemed a good way to help people and, quite honestly, because I was in so much pain myself. During the training period, I was ordained by the United Church of Christ to work in a church-sponsored community action agency on Staten Island. Within a year, the grant for the project ran out and was not renewed. With all other options gone, I threw myself into becoming a good psychotherapist, deciding that therapy would be my ministry.

After about seven years, when I was established as a Gestalt psychotherapist, I began to have vivid dreams about healing. I tried to push them away, but the Holy Spirit knows how to get the attention of a psychotherapist: Give her some dreams to chew on! Finally, I had to deal with them.

Even after exploring the dreams and admitting that God was asking me to look at healing prayer, I stalled for the better part of a year. Frankly, I was scared to death of the whole idea. Not only was I turned off by the simplistic style, the bad theology, and even worse psychology of TV healers, but I also was afraid of doing anything that would cause the church to reject me again. Nor did I want to tarnish my reputation as a therapist.

But those inner nudges kept pushing. It was clear that God was urging me to put my hands on someone and pray for healing. At last I did, but in such a way that I would not have to risk very much.

At the time, I was a part-time, Protestant chaplain at South Beach Psychiatric Center on Staten Island. I decided to find a patient there who was so psychotic that he or she would not know what I was doing. That way I would not have to make any false promises or explain anything theologically. If my prayers did not work—and I was reasonably sure they would not—no one would be the wiser.

The man I chose as guinea pig for this little experiment had been in the hospital for about a year. In that time he had spoken only in "word salad"—a speech pattern in which recognizable words are tossed together in a meaningless way. Unless asleep, he chattered almost constantly. I took him into an office and locked the door. I didn't want anyone to see this! As soon as I put my hands on his head, he stopped talking. I prayed a very simple prayer: "O God, please heal whatever caused this man to withdraw like this. In Jesus' name. Amen." As soon as I took my hands away he started jabbering again, and I breathed a sigh of relief. Good. It hadn't worked and I was off the hook.

When I was back on the ward several weeks later, a therapist practically pulled me into his office. "What did you do to that guy?" he demanded. I was too stunned to speak, as he told me that the man I had prayed for had begun talking normally that same afternoon. When asked what happened, the man reported that "the chaplain prayed for me." A week later the man was discharged.[1]

Was I awed and joyful that God had answered my prayer so dramatically? Only a little. The awe and joy came later. Mostly I felt cornered. It was inescapable; now I would have to explore this healing business further. And, in my "hardness of heart," I did not want to.

The healing of the psychotic man was hard to ignore, however. Very gingerly I began putting my hands on people to pray for their healing: other patients in the psychiatric hospital, some friends, one or two therapy clients. Interestingly enough, there were no more dramatic healings for quite a while. (Much later I was to conclude that dramatic, instantaneous healings are not the norm, but obviously they do happen on occasion.)

I noticed right away that most people seemed to be helped, but not totally healed, by my prayers. Sometimes a person was healed slowly over a period of weeks or months, but faster than the doctors had predicted. In other instances it seemed that not much changed at all for the person. Enough did happen, however, to con- vince me gradually that God was indeed using my prayers for healing.

My reaction to these experiences of healing was the dawning of a greatly renewed faith in the presence and love of Jesus. I saw him at work in the lives of hurting people, and I saw the transformations that resulted. As I observed all this, I myself was also being healed. I began to feel both joy and humility at being allowed to be part of God's healing work. At last I had found the ministry to which I was called! The training in psychotherapy seemed to be an important part of God's plan, not just a second-best vocational choice. The pain of the church's rejecting me slowly melted away.

As I was given a little faith and courage, the tentative beginnings blossomed into a new way of being a minister. Contrary to my expectations, I did not lose my clients or get branded as a kook by church folk. In fact the opposite happened. To my surprise, more people began to call for therapy appointments than before, and soon I was being asked to lead retreats. The United Methodist Church found a way to sponsor my transformed ministry and welcome me back to the denomination in which I had grown up. Fourteen years ago I began to teach ministers to work with Gestalt Pastoral Care, a mix of Gestalt psychotherapy, healing prayer, and spiritual companioning. Now, looking back, I see that for years I was being prepared to integrate these disciplines. I am convinced that people of faith are hungry to combine their psychotherapy with their spiritual journeys. Most Christian people are eager to experience healing prayer, and they desire a sense of God's presence in their lives.

## Bob's Story

My experience with healing prayer is closely tied to my emotional and spiritual growth and also to my profession as a seminary professor of New Testament.

I grew up in a church that surrounded me with love, and my decision to enter the ministry was a natural one. The seminary years were the most intellectually stimulating of my life. I developed a personal theology that was strong on reason and a scientific approach to the world. I have always been thankful for my academic training in theology, but looking back I know that what happened to me was similar to what happened to many like me. My theology became severed from its roots in prayer and from the practice of faith. My head and heart became alienated. Going on to graduate school, I found that the intense academic focus of years of study only heightened the split within me. While in many ways my life as a young adult was happy and fulfilling, I felt a lot of in nner distress. I sought and received help in psychotherapy. Clearly, my main emotional and spiritual work at this time was to achieve integration of these valuable but separated inner parts. A few years later, a family member experienced serious emotional difficulties and required lengthy hospitalization. All of us in the family suffered deeply. Sadly, but consistent with my intellectual training, I did not see the spiritual dimensions of this situation, nor did I offer more than perfunctory prayers for my distressed loved one.

While in this emotional state—outwardly functioning adequately but inwardly feeling fragmented—I gave some talks at a summer, weeklong pastors' retreat. At the same retreat, Tilda was leading what she called a "Workshop for Wounded Healers." I sat in as she worked with the pastors one-by-one in a group setting. The experience was revelatory. I saw people making rapid and significant breakthroughs in emotional, spiritual, and physical healing. I witnessed Tilda's powerful fusion of psychotherapy and healing prayer. In this setting I began—for the first time in years—to pray from the heart. (I now believe that for me this was the most important healing of all.)

Also, I was fascinated professionally by the way Tilda invited Jesus into people's experience as the agent of healing. What was the relation between the "historical Jesus" of my New Testament study and the directly experienced Jesus of what Tilda called "faith imagination"? The experience of this week moved me on many levels, stirring in me the need for healing in myself and my family.

The night I returned home from that retreat I had a dream in which I vividly experienced Jesus taking upon himself all the brokenness of my life. The painful memories of my life were still there, but their poison had drained away. I felt wonderfully free. The dream, plus all I had experienced at the pastors' retreat, demanded action. What should a professor do? The next term I offered a short course entitled "Exegetes and Healers in Dialogue." Cautiously I became the "exegete," eager to converse with anyone interested in spiritual healing. I was amazed at the response. Students and pastors gathered from everywhere, it seemed. Soon Tilda began to offer workshops through the seminary where I taught, and I continued experiencing her work. Together we began to offer regular workshops on healing prayer for pastors, seminarians, and laypersons. In this way I was responding professionally to a call to be an interpreter of, and advocate for, Christian healing in mainline churches.

My personal experience of the healing love of God has continued too, although I am very much a novice in practice. Over the past few years I have discovered in myself and in others the surprising ways that God works in us when we open ourselves through prayer.

What I am most thankful for in this spiritual adventure is my own renewed awareness of the reality of our loving, healing God, alive in me and in the world.

## *Healing: The Church's Story*

Our personal experiences of healing are shaped by our individual personalities, life experiences, and senses of call. Each person has a unique story to tell of the ways in which God addresses her or his needs and gifts.

But all our stories together are something more. They are signs of a broader movement that has been present in the church down through the ages and is enjoying a widespread renewal in churches in our own day. Twenty years ago, it was a rare church that had regular healing services, but today services of healing are sprouting up everywhere. Surely the Holy Spirit is inviting the church to a revival of interest in healing.

If spiritual healing has always had some part in the church's life, why does it need to be "revived" in our day? What happened to the church's healing ministry in Christendom over the centuries? And what factors have led to the revival of interest in healing in recent years? In order to put our own approach to Christian healing in a broader perspective, let us touch on a few highlights of the story of healing in the historic Christian church.[2]

For the first two or three centuries of the church's existence, Christian writers maintained the dominant New Testament perspectives on healing. Speaking for the times, Origen (third century) wrote, "the name of Jesus can still remove distractions from the minds of men, and expel demons, and also take away diseases."[3] In the Eastern church such belief flourished for centuries and exists today in an Orthodox service of healing based on an ancient liturgy.[4] As for the Western church, Morton Kelsey identifies three reasons why healing was generally discounted in the Western church from the Middle Ages until now.[5]

First, the early theologians of the West began to downplay and even discourage the gift of healing, under the impact of heightened senses of human depravity and of divine punishment. Illness was seen either as punishment for sin or as a means to prepare the sufferer for the soul's salvation. The soul and body were separated and associated with good and evil, respectively. This-worldly existence in physical bodies was a source of suspicion or denial. As an illustration of this trend, the ancient practice of anointing for healing gradually became a service of last rites, a preparation of the soul for death.

Augustine of Hippo (fourth century) shared this suspicion of Christian healing, teaching that miraculous healings were marks of the apostolic age and not for his own day. Yet late in his life, partly because he witnessed some spectacular healings at the altar of the church while he was presiding at worship, Augustine revised his views and "instituted the recording and attesting of miracles" in his diocese.[6]

Second, probably the most important factor in the decline of healing in the Western church was the rise of rationalism, and its flowering in the movement known as Scholasticism. The highly rationalized theological system of Thomas Aquinas (thirteenth century) allowed no place for religious healing or the exercise of the spiritual gifts mentioned by Paul. Jesus performed miracles, he argued, in order to prove his teaching and to demonstrate his divinity. Physical healing was meant to lead to spiritual healing: "By how much a soul is of more account than a body, by so much is the forgiving of sins a greater work than healing the body; but because the one is unseen He does the lesser and more manifest thing in order to prove the greater and more unseen."[7]

The Protestant Reformation of the sixteenth century did not entirely break with this rationalism. Both Martin Luther and John

Calvin, perhaps reacting against some of the superstitious claims of the day and against the Roman Catholic sacrament of anointing, argued that miracles of healing were only for the time of the early church. Calvin wrote,

> [The] gift of healing, like the rest of the miracles, . . . has vanished away to make the new preaching of the gospel marvelous forever. Therefore, even if we grant to the full that anointing was a sacrament of those powers which were then administered by the hands of the apostles, it now has nothing to do with us, to whom the administering of such powers has not been committed.[8]

Luther also denied the gift of healing for his own day but lived, as Kelsey says, "to see his friend Melanchthon visibly brought from the point of death through his own prayers." Luther once wrote in a letter that "a cabinetmaker here was . . . afflicted with madness and we cured him by prayer in Christ's name."[9] Apparently Luther's practice, like Augustine's, was not entirely consistent with his theory!

The Enlightenment of the eighteenth century made the theological climate even less congenial to belief in spiritual healing. Theological voices tended to be either hostile or at best guarded in their estimations of the ability or the will of God to heal through nonmedical means. To this day, silence on the subject is the typical reaction in most mainstream theological circles.

Third, turning to healing in popular religious practice, we find a different situation. In ancient and medieval times, people often turned to healing through such means as oils, prayers to saints and the use of their relics, sleeping in sacred shrines, and receiving the prayers of those deemed especially holy. Shrines such as Lourdes attest both to the persistence of the gift of healing in the church and to its unfortunate relegation to the margins of church life.

In virtually every age of the church there have been those whose ministries were accompanied by healing, from St. Francis Xavier and St. Vincent de Paul on the Roman Catholic side to George Fox, John Wesley, and Johann Christoph Blumhardt on the Protestant.[10]

In nineteenth and twentieth century America many names are associated with ministries of healing, such as Mary Baker Eddy, Kathryn Kuhlman, and Oral Roberts. Perhaps their theologies or ministries have been associated with controversy in part because mainstream Christian tradition has lacked its own vital theology of healing, one that could have assimilated whatever true insights and gifts such figures possessed.

The church's story of healing leaves an impression of lost opportunities. Theology and practice have not supported and enriched each other as they should. At times both have departed from the biblical heritage. Yet the gift of healing has persisted, often unfortunately removed from the church's sacramental and corporate life.

As we bring the church's story up-to-date, how do we account for the renewal of Christian healing in our day? Among the many factors that could be mentioned we select three.

1. We are in a period when the very models by which we understand our world are in transition. In fields as diverse as physics and politics, biology and religion, a profound shift of perception is taking place, from viewing the world as a mechanism to seeing it more as an organism, from compartmentalizing reality to seeing things whole. Accompanying this shift in perception is a deepened appreciation for the ways in which emotions, body, and mind influence each other. Christians are recognizing that their own heritage contains practical wisdom about health and wholeness that is of astonishing contemporary relevance.

2. Under the influence of Postmodernism, the Enlightenment confidence in human reason is eroding in our day. As a result, in both academic theology and popular faith, one may find a greater openness to the transcendent and spiritual. Ironically, the rationalism that once blandly dismissed accounts of unexplained healings is itself now seen as naive and culture-bound.

3. Cultural developments aside, many Christians interpret the gentle renewal of healing in our day as a sign that the Holy Spirit is at work in the church and in the world. This is evident in dramatic ways in the ministries of specially gifted people such as Agnes Sanford and Francis MacNutt. More important, the Spirit's work is evident in the lives of countless believers who have experienced healing in the name of Jesus, and in the ministries of countless others who have allowed God to use them in acts of healing, great and small.

It may be misleading to speak of a "revival" of Christian healing in our time. Christians have always prayed for healing. What is relatively new today is that the idea of healing is finding a more fertile cultural soil than in the past and is reaching a broader audience of people, who are aware of their own need for healing and are willing to trust God's will for their wholeness.

Could it be that the best parts of the church's story of healing are yet to be told?

## Beyond the Stereotypes

Since beginning our own explorations of healing ministry, we have seen many persons healed or helped through the laying on of hands and other types of prayer. In our experience, although God deals with each person uniquely (and often in surprising ways), certain patterns recur.

1. People are healed in ways that involve every level of their being: body, mind, spirit, and emotions. It is often the case that the healing received is different from—and deeper than—the healing prayed for. Those who pray for healing learn to expect that God will work, but often in utterly surprising ways. In healing prayer we have indeed learned to expect the unexpected.

2. Although it may not happen instantly, after prayer healing frequently occurs faster than medically predicted.

3. When someone is healed through prayer, his or her knowledge of the love of God grows, a knowledge that is personal and experiential and leads to joy. Most people, in addition, find a great freedom to stretch out their hands to others as lovers and healers in the name of Jesus.

Consider the story of Mary, a first-grade teacher and Roman Catholic nun for over forty years. Her beautiful story of healing points to the surprising and holistic way in which God works.

## Sister Mary's Story

Mary had developed such painful ankles that she found it difficult to teach. Her doctors thought perhaps she suffered from a form of arthritis, but they were unable to help her very much.

Mary's predicament deeply troubled her. She loved teaching and considered it the ministry to which she was called. Her distress was compounded by her lifelong painful shyness. What could she do if she was not able to be with her "little people," the only ones with whom she was really comfortable?

When her suffering became evident to some members of her parish, they invited Mary to attend a healing prayer group in her church. At first she refused, fearing she might have to talk in front of everyone. Worse yet, if the parishioners prayed for her, she would be the center of attention. And then there were all those hands that would touch her. . . .

In the end, her friends won out. Reluctantly, she went to the meeting and, just as she had feared, found herself in the middle of a group of people. They prayed for her, their hands on her ankles: "Jesus, please heal Sister Mary's ankles. . . . Hear our prayer, O God." God heard; but God did not heal Mary's ankles. Instead a wonderfully funny thing happened. As the group prayed for her ankles, her ear that had been nearly deaf since childhood suddenly opened, allowing her to hear with that ear for the first time in many years. Amid the laughter and the tears that followed, any illusions that the group could predict what God would do quickly melted away.

The next week Mary did not need urging to attend the healing group. Once again the group prayed for her ankles, and once again she experienced healing, but not in her ankles. Instead, the arthritis in her arm improved.

This went on week after week for several months. Each time the group prayed for Mary's ankles, some minor ache or pain would vanish or improve. Many times the group would end in laughter at the peculiar way God seemed to be working. However, Mary was certain that God was indeed at work, and the small physical improvements kept her coming back.

During this time, God was working marvelously with Mary in other ways. She became deeply aware that God loved her. Of course Mary already "knew" this, and she had taught her first graders that God is love. But now for the first time in her life Mary felt God's passionate, tender love. God was no longer a demanding father ready with punishments if she did not work hard to please him, but one who delighted in her. As Jesus became more real to her as friend as well as savior, Mary's shyness gradually diminished. She even found herself reading the Old Testament lesson at Sunday worship in front of hundreds of people, something she would not have dreamed of doing only a few months before.

But here is the enigma: Mary still had painful ankles. They had improved only a little after months of prayer. One day Mary was asked why she thought the pain in her ankles persisted. She replied: "My ankles were the bait that enticed me to pray for healing in the first place. The continued pain kept me coming back so that God could heal me in ways I didn't even know to pray for. I couldn't have imagined the depth of this healing and how it involved so much of me. Just think of what I would have missed if my ankles had been healed that first night. God had something much more profound in mind for me than just my ankles."

Then her eyes twinkled and she smiled her wonderful smile. "Anyway, don't say my ankles weren't healed. Just say they aren't healed yet." She went on to say that she had begun to sense a new call to be a chaplain to some of the older sisters in her community who were in poor health. She was looking forward to developing a new ministry in that direction.

Mary's story points to some important truths about Christian healing, what it is and what it is not.

## What Christian Healing Is Not

1. *Christian healing is not magic. It is not manipulating God to do what we want; rather, it is surrendering to God's healing work in us.*

2. *Christian faith for healing is not a prediction of what God will do; it is simple trust that God loves us and is at work in us already.*

3. *Christian healing is not to be sought as a spiritual thrill for the healer or the person healed but is a way to grow as a Christian.*

4. *Christian healing is not proof that we are faithful or holy but a sign of God's love.*

## What Christian Healing Is

*Christian healing is a process that involves the totality of our being— body, mind, emotion, spirit, and our social context—and that directs us toward becoming the person God is calling us to be at every stage of our living and our dying. When-ever we are truly open to God, some kind of healing takes place, because God yearns to bring us to wholeness. Through prayer and the laying on of hands, through confession, anointing, the sacraments, and other means of grace, Jesus meets us in our brokenness and pain and there loves, transforms, forgives, redeems, resurrects, and heals. Jesus does this in God's way, in God's time, and according to God's loving purpose for each person.*

*Because the Holy Spirit is continually at work in each of us, pushing us toward wholeness, the process of healing is like removing sticks and leaves from a stream until the water runs clear. If we simply get out of the way of the Lord's work in us, we can trust that we are being led to the particular kind of wholeness God wills for us.*

*Very often the results of our healing are increased faith in God and a new empowerment to love and serve others. Frequently we find that the very thing that caused our greatest brokenness becomes transformed into our own unique giftedness.*

*In the following pages we will refer often to this statement of what healing is. Much of what follows explains and illustrates this understanding of healing.*

## CHAPTER TWO

# Frequently Asked Questions about Healing

I n our own explorations of healing we have learned the importance of honoring our questions. Both in ourselves and in the people with whom we work, questions inevitably arise. How could it be otherwise in an area as personal and sometimes controversial as healing prayer? We have learned too that even tough and nagging questions need not deter us from praying for healing. When questions are taken seriously they can lead to deep understanding and commitment. The questions raised in this chapter are the ones we hear most frequently. They are also the ones we ourselves have often asked and continue to ask. Let's begin by considering the importance of questioning.

*Honest questions are important because they can lead to deeper engagement.* In all areas of Christian life, questions are an important part of a thoughtful and growing faith. Often the more serious and seemingly radical the question, the greater its potential for deep and life-changing insight. And what is true of the life of faith in general is especially true of healing prayer. The Spirit can use our questions and doubts to lead us into deeper understandings of the healing process. We do not have to fear our questions.

However, *questions can be used to avoid personal involvement.* Sometimes people ask lots of questions as a defense against taking healing prayer seriously and personally. Understand, this is not necessarily willful avoidance. We humans naturally tend to resist challenges to long-held beliefs, or the opening of tender wounds, or even the gentle invitation to change old ways. We can use questions to keep change at arm's length. All the more reason to face our questions openly and prayerfully.

The questions in this chapter are grouped by theme, with some inevitable overlapping. Of course it is scarcely possible in a few sentences to provide pat "answers" to serious questions. Take the following discussion as the starting point for your own reflections. As you read you may want to reframe or add to the questions, in order to make them your own.

## A "Modern, Scientific" Orientation

1. *Isn't nonmedical healing just a result of the power of suggestion or positive thinking, an example of the "placebo effect"?*

There is no doubt that the power of suggestion is very great in the realm of healing, as it is in most other areas of human experience. Most of us have had some personal experience in which we responded physically to mental or emotional suggestion. We ease headaches and backaches by the power of positive thoughts or positive imaging. Many people have dramatic stories of the effects of positive suggestion upon serious illness. The "placebo effect" is real. In our day scientific studies as well as spiritual writings testify to the reality of body-mind connections and the power of the mind to affect the body.[1]

This is all to the good and fully in keeping with Christian faith. We Christians affirm that God works through human psychological processes. But to say healing is merely psychological, as if our minds and emotions were not a realm of divine activity, would imply a limitation upon God. The fact that our bodies and minds are so intimately connected shows us that a purely materialistic account of human life is not adequate to explain how we are "fearfully and wonderfully made" (Ps. 139:14). So it is erroneous to try to explain away inner human experience, such as experiences of healing, as "merely" psychological. Reducing religious experience to psychological terms impoverishes religious faith.

More than that, we affirm that God is active in and through people's lives, working lovingly and sometimes powerfully to move them toward becoming the persons God created them to be. As we begin to act on this faith, our thinking shifts from explaining God away toward a positive affirmation of God's lively healing activity in us.

*2. Can you prove it? Can you ever say for sure that it was prayer or supernatural intervention that effected a specific healing?*

Let us be clear that in talking about spiritual healing we are not dealing with the realm of empirical proof. By hard scientific standards, much of the evidence for healings would be considered anecdotal (but what anecdotes!). Yet we affirm the importance of those areas of life that are not subject to proof, areas where the human element is paramount. This includes most of what marks us as human—our values, personal relations, and religious experience.

Although we imply no devaluing of science and technology, it seems that a strictly scientific mind-set can shut one off from positive experiences of healing prayer. What we suggest to those who are inclined toward skepticism is that they conduct an experiment: experiment with laying their skepticism aside for a while—imagine putting it on a shelf where it can be retrieved later—so that another way of experiencing reality, another way of knowing, may be allowed to come to the fore. Of course, one need not accept every miraculous claim that comes along. But just imagine the difference between responding, "How can people believe such things!" and asking, "Do I sense the love and power of God at work in this situation?"

3. *Shouldn't we just put our trust in modern medicine? Isn't it dangerous to suggest that people can get along without medical science?*

It is important to be clear that healing prayer is not an *alternative* to medical care. An incarnational Christian faith affirms that *the art and science of medicine is a good gift of God, one of the ways in which God heals.* Forms of religious healing that make the willingness to give up medicine a test of one's faith are based on a theology that, we believe, artificially separates the mind and spirit from the body and misinterprets certain passages from the Bible.

That said, should Christians trust in modern medicine alone? Put that way, of course Christians should not trust in anything alone other than God! Trusting in God the healer, then, involves employing all the means of healing God has provided: good physical and mental self-care, medical science, and the spiritual means of healing given in the Christian tradition—prayer, laying on hands and anointing, public worship, and the sacraments. How strange it would seem for those who believe in God *not* to draw on all the means of healing God provides!

*Healing prayer and a scientific outlook.* Behind these initial questions lies a deeper question about whether God truly acts in the world. Such skepticism is deeply ingrained in modern culture and affects most of us, religious and nonreligious alike. The theological and philosophical issues are complex. But a scientific view of healing can be broadened and enriched when we acknowledge three things. First, scientists themselves today advocate a much more open view of the connections between the physical and the nonphysical than laypersons in science usually realize.[2] Christians who continue to think in terms of a sharp separation of body and mind are actually lagging behind their secular counterparts. Second, some contemporary models of Christian theology are breaking down the dualism of earlier times, offering resources for a solid theological grounding for the practice of healing prayer.[3] Third, and most important, *the practice of healing prayer will always be something experienced before it is understood, known by the heart before it is grasped by the mind.* A scientific outlook, legitimate and appropriate in itself, need not be a block to exploring healing prayer. What are needed are a willingness to experiment, an open mind and heart, and trust in God, our good creator and healer.

## Resignation to God's Will or to "Fate"

4. *Should we presume to tamper with nature by praying for healing, since disease and death are natural?*

Death is indeed entirely natural and can even be seen as a kindly part of the larger cycle of life. We know too that death can be the ultimate healing for persons who have suffered long, wasting illness. On occasion, well-meant prayers for a loved one's healing can actually seem to stand in the way of the release of a timely death. Always, we need to exercise wisdom and discernment to help us know how to pray in a given situation. (Discernment will be discussed more completely in chapter 3.)

None of this suggests, however, that we ought not to pray for healing, only that we ought to bring into our prayers for healing a discernment of and openness to God's timely, loving will for the particular person, a will infinitely wiser and more perfect than our own. Jesus said, "If you then, who are evil, know how to give good gifts to your children, how much more will your Father in heaven give good things to those who ask him!" (Matt. 7:11). These simple yet profound words assure us that God does want us to be whole and can be trusted to bestow the kind of healing that is right for the moment, even if it be the healing of death.

*5. Shouldn't we pray that God's will be done and leave it at that? Isn't it presumptuous to pray for more?*

There is a kind of religious fatalism, a stoic submission to the implacable will of God, that is deeply ingrained in our heritage. This attitude appears to be genuinely faithful, and sometimes truly may be so, but it needs to be examined carefully.

When our ancestors buried their dead, they sometimes consoled themselves with the words of Job, "The LORD gave and the LORD hath taken away; blessed be the name of the LORD" (Job 1:21, KJV). They were tapping into a strain of biblical faith that saw Yahweh's hand alike in health and illness, healing and death. "I kill and I make alive; I wound and I heal; and no one can deliver from my hand" (Deut. 32:39).[4] It is not surprising that many of us, especially in times of personal tragedy, resort to this faithful-sounding fatalism. It can be a way of trying to make some sense of what otherwise seems inexplicably tragic.

But there are other, less fatalistic, voices in the biblical tradition that highlight God as the source of healing and wholeness. Recall Yahweh's promise to Israel at the outset of their wandering in the wilderness: "I am the LORD who heals you" (Exod. 15:26). Think also of the prophet Elijah's miraculous raising of the widow's son (1 Kings 17:17-24) and Elisha's raising of the Shunammite woman's son (2 Kings 4:18-37; see also 5:1-14).

Of course it is Jesus who especially embodies God's compassion for those in need. Often in Jesus' healings, those who come or are brought for healing demonstrate their great desire and need for healing. Jesus receives and honors their desire and responds as we believe God responds, by meeting their needs and granting their requests.

Jesus' Gethsemane prayer perfectly epitomizes the faithful attitude: "Abba, Father, for you all things are possible; remove this cup from me; yet, not what I want, but what you want" (Mark 14:36).[5] Jesus felt free to ask for his heart's desire; he was then ready to give over his own wish to the will of God. *There is a great difference between two kinds of "surrender"—giving up and giving over.*

Fatalism is giving up. By contrast, without presuming to impose our wills upon God, we seek in our prayers to *give* ourselves *over* to what God wants to do in and through us. Such an attitude honors God's will above all but is not fatalistic.

### 6. *Isn't it true that healing was for biblical times, but not for now?*

Some traditional Christian theology has taught that history is divided into epochs, or "dispensations."[6] In this view, miracles were associated with the dispensation of the founding of the church but are not part of God's work today. Recently the number of people holding this belief has declined considerably.

The dispensationalists' view on healing is mistaken for two reasons. First, it is not biblical. Nowhere in the Bible is the phenomenon of healing limited to a particular time. On the contrary, the Bible gives the strong impression that part of God's unchanging character is to desire wholeness for every creature. Confident of that, we pray for healing.

Second, God continues to heal, despite dispensationalism! As we saw in chapter 1, healing has been a part of the historic church's ministry since the close of the apostolic age. Also, we are experiencing a resurgence of healing prayer in our day. Among charismatics and mainstream believers, high church Episcopalians and free-church Mennonites, pietists and activists, more and more people are finding encouragement to pray for healing. Experience shows that healing is most assuredly for today.

## What Prayer Is and Is Not

7. *Aren't we flirting with magic when we link human prayer with divine action in a cause-and-effect way?*

Magic is the human attempt to affect or control supernatural forces by natural means, as when a person wears a charm to ward off evil spirits. Simplistic, magiclike prayers for instantaneous cures have little to do with what we understand about prayer as Jesus modeled it and as practiced by the saints of the church. In praying for healing, we do not imagine we are coercing the divine will, or directing God, or informing God of things God would otherwise not have known.

Prayer is not directing God but directing ourselves toward God; not informing God, but conforming ourselves to God. Led by the Holy Spirit, in prayer we listen to God in the faith that we may receive and channel God's limitless love. The heart of healing prayer is discerning how God is working for healing in a particular situation, and conforming our prayers to the movement of God's Spirit. This is not magic, but it is mystery, the mystery of entering into communion with God through the Holy Spirit.

8. *If God wants to heal, why can't God just do it? Why are our prayers necessary?*

Sometimes God does seem to work quite independently of any known human prayer or intercession. Once we open our eyes to

God's healing activity, we can expect to be utterly surprised by what we see. At such times we may conclude there seems to be nothing that God cannot do. More often our experience is that God is waiting for our prayers and using our prayers to heal. The flowing, grace-filled relationship between creature and creator is mysterious indeed. Our experience is that God desires our prayers and does sometimes seem to wait for us to respond to grace. Though it would not be right to insist that our prayers are necessary, it does seem right to respond to the divine invitation to pray for healing, trusting that God will use these prayers for good in ways we do not control and may not fully grasp. In short, we pray out of obedience to the call to pray.

## Social and Ethical Reservations about Healing Prayer

9. *Isn't it selfish to pray for myself when other people are so much worse off?*

It may sound altruistic, even heroic, when someone says this. We may be tempted to admire their selflessness. But fear of being selfish can be a cop-out from taking care of ourselves or of letting ourselves be cared for. It may even mask feelings of unworthiness or guilt. Perhaps we feel that a part of us is unworthy of God's love.

God has enough love to go around! How can it be selfish to value ourselves even as God values us? It is this *appropriate self-regard* that motivates us to ask God to make us the whole persons we are intended to be. However we may feel about ourselves, praying for our own healing is a response to a call from God to be on the journey toward wholeness. On that journey, as we experience healing we become more available agents in the healing of others.

**10. *Isn't an emphasis on healing narcissistic, just a form of religion suited to the "me generation"?***

Narcissus was the beautiful youth who fell in love with his own image. Intense self-involvement is undoubtedly a mark of our culture, one Christians need to resist. Although we naturally tend toward self-involvement during illness, it would be unfortunate if an emphasis upon healing prayer were to play upon and heighten that narcissism. Unfortunately, some forms of healing ministry seem to evoke this attitude. "Heal me, heal me," the petitioner seems to cry.

Desiring to be healed need not be narcissistic when healing is seen as growing toward becoming the whole person God intends us to be. Focusing on God's will for us should help us distinguish between appropriate and excessive self-love.

**11. *Isn't the focus on healing too individualistic, separating people from community and diverting them from social responsibility?***

Reflecting the individualism of American culture, some contemporary expressions of healing do seem to be terribly individualistic. Some forms of so-called New Age healing and television faith-healing, for example, focus upon individual healing as an end in itself. Some persons involved in healing show little regard for anything beyond themselves. Most books about healing make no mention of the social dimensions of human life.

Must it be this way? Is it inevitable that justice ministries and healing ministries must go their separate ways? Are these simply two alternative versions of the faith? These are crucial questions for the mainstream church today. Our conviction is that no understanding of healing prayer is adequate that tends to take individuals out of community or that separates individual wholeness from social wholeness. To put the matter positively, *the church's healing ministry should always address both the social order and the lives of individuals; authentic Christian healing will be both social and individual in its impact.*[7]

Our conviction is rooted in several affirmations. First, Jesus healed not simply because he felt compassion for individuals, though he surely was compassionate (see Mark 1:41; 8:2). He healed because he thereby brought the rule of God—that is, the active power and presence of God—into the lives of the people as a whole. As with Jesus' healing ministry, so also with the church's healing ministry today. Beyond the love and compassion we naturally feel for those who suffer, we pray for healing because we believe that God will use our prayers to establish the divine rule not only in individuals but also in all creation. One of the things that makes Christian healing "Christian" is just this corporate framework of God's healing work. From this point of view, there can be no exclusive focus upon individual healing.

Second, the more we grow toward wholeness, the more we will be sensitized to the needs of the world around us and equipped for doing God's will and work in the world. Healing of body or mind that does not issue in a deeper commitment to peace and justice is only a partial healing at best.

Third, we are called to pray not only for the healing of individuals but also for the healing of social institutions. To put the matter more strongly, ritually encountering social evil (the modern-day social equivalent of Jesus' casting out demons) is part of the church's healing ministry.[8]

In short, we need to overcome the false and misleading separation sometimes made between individually spiritual and socially active forms of faith. In Christian healing prayer, such a distinction may sometimes be encountered in practice but needs to be transcended.

## *Timidity, Fear, or Resignation*

12. *Why pray for healing? I tried it and it didn't work. When your time comes, it comes.*

Such utterances may express a variety of attitudes and emotions. Sometimes they can be used as excuses for not opening up to the possibility of healing. Strange as it may seem, sometimes people prefer the limitation or illness they know to the unknown changes healing would bring. Jesus' question to the man paralyzed thirty-eight years is pertinent: "Do you want to be made well?" (John 5:6). Sometimes people give up, resigning themselves to their afflictions or limitations. Thus they relinquish the initiative to act on their own behalf or to let the Spirit intercede for them (Romans 8:26). In such instances we are dealing not with rational challenges to the idea of healing but with faintheartedness or fear. The appropriate response is to kindle trust in God the healer who desires wholeness and is able to heal.

Sometimes a feeling of resignation arises from the mistaken idea that healing should come virtually instantaneously in response to a single "prayer of faith," as with the person who attends one healing service to cure a serious malady. When healing does not happen quickly, the person loses hope. Hence the timid conclusion, "I tried it and it didn't work."

Recall the definition of healing in chapter 1: healing is a *process*. While sometimes the process can be very fast, virtually instantaneous, that is not the usual experience. And if we were to stop after one or two or three prayers, we could be cutting ourselves off from what God wants to do in our lives. One-time faith-healing is not comparable to the process of healing inaugurated when we open ourselves to the ongoing activity of the Holy Spirit.

## The Theory and Practice of Healing Prayer

13. *Does a person have to have faith to be healed? Some seem to be healed without it.*

The short answer to this question is no. God can get around our lack of faith. But because few issues are as troublesome as the relation of faith to healing, a fuller discussion is required.

In the movement popularly known as faith healing—a term not used in this book to describe healing prayer—a harmful, unethical, and false reasoning is employed:

> If you have enough faith, you will be healed.
> If you are not healed, it is because you do not have enough faith.

This simplistic formula is harmful because in effect it "blames the victim" for any apparent failure to be healed, adding guilt to the burdens the sufferer already bears. This formula is also unethical. The "healer" who employs it is often surrounded with an aura of power and holiness. If healing does not happen, all the blame falls on the one seeking healing; the healer is immune from scrutiny. It is not surprising that such healers are sometimes tempted to abuse their gifts.

We believe the faith-healing formula is also theologically wrong. It appears to coerce God, in effect saying, "If I have enough faith, then God must do what I want." Such an idea borders on magic. Also, it expresses an inadequate understanding of what faith is, in the biblical sense. What is "enough" faith? Is faith something quantifiable? In contrast, biblical faith is more a matter of *trusting in* God's love and power than *believing* that a certain result will be achieved. Yes, we can have "little" faith or "great" faith (see Matt. 14:31; 15:28), but that is more a measure of the *quality and complete-*

*ness of our dependence upon God* than upon what or how much we believe.

Finally, the faith-healing formula tends to shift the focus to my believing rather than to the One whom I trust. Faith then becomes "faith in faith" rather than "faith in God."[9]

While we have identified this linking of faith and healing with the movement called "faith healing," in fact this way of thinking occurs quite commonly, especially when people are under the stress of serious illness.

A tragic illustration of the harm and error of the faith-healing formula is the experience of a deeply disturbed man who, on his twelfth suicide attempt, lost both legs after throwing himself in the path of a subway train. During his recovery he was convinced by a faith healer that God could grow his legs back, if he just had enough faith. To one already deeply depressed and mentally unstable, this approach simply wreaked further emotional havoc.

## Faith and Healing in the Gospels

Do you have to have faith to be healed? Let us explore the question more deeply from the perspective of the words and deeds of Jesus in the Gospels. There we find material that seems both to challenge and to confirm our approach.

Undoubtedly the most challenging biblical material are sayings of Jesus that express a strong link between faith and answered prayer. Consider these sayings of Jesus:

> For truly I tell you, if you have faith the size of a mustard seed, you will say to this mountain, "Move from here to there," and it will move;

and nothing will be impossible for you (Matt. 17:20; see also Luke 17:5).

Have faith in God. Truly, I tell you, if you say to this mountain, "Be taken up and thrown into the sea," and if you do not doubt in your heart, but believe that what you say will come to pass, it will be done for you. So I tell you, whatever you ask for in prayer, believe that you have received it, and it will be yours (Mark 11:22-24; see also Matt. 17:14-21; Luke 9:37-43).

I will do whatever you ask in my name, so that the Father may be glorified in the Son. If in my name you ask me for anything, I will do it (John 14:13-14; see also Matt. 7:7-11; 18:19-20).

In addition, faith is mentioned as a factor in healing in seven of the eighteen separate healing miracles of the Gospels (excluding parallel accounts). For example, three times Jesus says, "Your faith has made you well," or "According to your faith let it be done to you" (Matt. 9:29; Mark 5:34; 10:52; Luke 17:19; see also Matt. 8:10, 13; Mark 2:5; 5:36).

Faith is named as a factor in two of the five separate accounts of Jesus casting out demons. He says to the Canaanite woman who pleads on behalf of her daughter, "Woman, great is your faith! Let it be done for you as you wish" (Matt. 15:28; but compare Mark 7:28-29). And to the father who says on behalf of his son, "if you are able to do anything, have pity on us and help us," Jesus replies, "If you are able!—All things can be done for the one who believes" (Mark 9:22-23).[10]

What are we to make of this evidence? Clearly Jesus spoke with astonishing boldness about what God is able to do through people who trust in God utterly. Nevertheless, it would be a mistake to turn these sayings into a rigid faith-healing system. First, we recall that hyperbole, or exaggerated speech, was a characteristic trait of

Jesus' speech. Remember the camel and the needle's eye, and the threat of hell for calling someone a fool (Matt. 19:24; 5:22). Such sayings were not meant to be taken literally as spiritual laws. Hyperbole was a device whereby Jesus seized his hearers' imaginations and pierced their defenses.[11]

Second, we recognize that these bold utterances ought not be lifted out as proof texts, that is, taken in isolation from the whole biblical message about the interaction of divine power and human freedom. Again and again in scripture we encounter poignant stories of people of great faith who endured much suffering and did not receive the healing they desired.[12]

Recognizing the limitations of these bold sayings of Jesus, we still may be called to bolder faith and expectations than we are accustomed to. We would then take these sayings seriously and faithfully, without making of them a simplistic formula.

It is important to note that *about two-thirds of the Gospel healing stories lack any mention of faith.* Probably some came to Jesus with confidence in him, like the leper who knelt before Jesus and said, "If you choose, you can make me clean" (Mark 1:40). Often, however, those whom Jesus healed were not people of faith but just happened to be in the right place at the right time, like the man in the synagogue (Mark 1:23-26), or the man beside the pool (John 5:2-9), or the man born blind (John 9). This broader survey of Jesus' healings is evidence that the faith-healing formula is not justified on biblical grounds.

We conclude that faith, understood as reliance upon God and trust in Jesus the healer, is profoundly important in healing prayer, as it is in every aspect of our lives. We are called to become ever bolder and more radical in our reliance upon God. But to insist on the strict connection between healing and faith is not consistent with the Gospel portraits of Jesus' healings. Perpetuating the faith-healing formula is neither good theology, good ethics, nor good pastoral care.

These conclusions are supported by our experience in healing ministry. In the actual practice of praying with others for healing, it seems that sometimes God does wait for faith. Often, as the one seeking healing enters more deeply into a loving and trusting relationship with God, then healing begins. Again, this is no pat formula. What we continue to see and marvel at is how God can get around our little faith.

### 14. *Why are some people not healed?*

This is probably the most frequently asked and the most wrenching question about healing prayer. We have already expressed our belief that whenever we open ourselves to God's healing, some kind of healing takes place, though it may not be in the way we expect. This bold position rests upon a simple trust in the character of God, in God's loving disposition to give good things to those who ask (Matt. 7:11). But its very boldness creates pressure to explain the common experience that our prayers are often not answered in recognizable ways. Some theological and practical considerations may be helpful in reflecting on this question.

Theologically, we acknowledge that because we are human and not God, we are unable finally to penetrate the mystery of divine being. A full and satisfactory answer to the question of why particular people are not healed can never be given. Further, we know ourselves to be creatures subject to the contingencies of both natural evil (such as accident, disease, and genetic flaw) and moral evil (such as idolatry and addiction of every kind). We differ in our understandings of how God acts, and thus in our understandings of the means of healing available to us. Some will emphasize God's self-limited power; others will emphasize the limitlessly healing power of divine love; and so on. We will thus tend to have different opinions about why some are not healed.

There are also practical considerations. Factors within the realm of human freedom can inhibit or detract from healing. Perhaps in a given instance the people who pray have not accurately discerned how or what to pray for.[13] Or, the one needing healing may be blocking the work of the Spirit in any number of ways: by holding onto resentment or being unwilling to forgive, by unconsciously preferring to stay with the suffering because it is familiar, or by continuing the unhealthy lifestyle that has caused illness. Or, perhaps, this is not the time or these are not the people to effect the healing that seems to be needed.[14]

Affirming God's disposition to bless us always, we recognize that these are very real factors that may inhibit the healing process. When we discover, in ourselves or in others, the presence of such a factor, then of course that becomes the focus of our prayer.

15. *What if I pray and healing doesn't happen? Is it because I'm a bad person or don't have enough faith?*

This is the personal and existential form of the last question. Hospital chaplains and pastoral counselors remark on the common human tendency to find a reason, or a scapegoat, for illness and for the apparent failure of healing prayer. Many religiously inclined people in particular voice feelings of guilt or low self-esteem under the stress of suffering and illness.

The feeling that one is a "bad person" whose unanswered prayers are God's punishment is itself a crippling emotional condition that calls out for healing prayer. To be freed from such self-judging feelings and to accept God's unconditional love are two of the greatest forms of healing anyone can receive.

Do illness and the withholding of healing imply divine punishment for being a "bad person"? Put that way, the issue is clear. We do not believe illness is a punishment from God, nor do we believe God withholds healing in order to punish sin. Neither an individual's cancer, nor chronic depression, nor HIV positive or AIDS, nor any other disease, is sent by God as punishment. Although, as we have seen, some biblical texts speak of both healing and illness as sent by God, or speak of illness as being brought on by sin, these are not the major thrust of biblical faith about illness, especially as seen in the words and deeds of Jesus. Jesus specifically refused to speculate on the causes of illness or evil (see Luke 13:1-5; John 9:2). Instead, he simply touched the sick and healed them of their diseases, and in that way he embodied the compassion of God.

Finally, we need to remind ourselves to let God set the healing agenda, instead of presuming we know what needs to happen or what healing will look like in a specific instance. Also, we need to exercise careful discernment in framing our prayers for healing, discernment sensitive to the movement of the Spirit and the needs of each unique situation.

16. *What if I pray for another's healing and the person isn't healed? Couldn't this make the person feel unworthy or abandoned by God? I don't want to "blame the victim."*

This question is motivated by care and concern for another. Just as medical caregivers want above all to avoid doing harm to their patients, so those praying for others do not want to make matters worse by glibly creating hopes that are not fulfilled. Some sensitive pastors hesitate to pray for healing because they do not want to create hopes that will remain unfulfilled in people who are already hurting. Such responsible pastoral concern is valid and commendable. However, healing prayer cannot harm and, in fact, richly contributes to good pastoral care when we keep in mind that (1) God wants people to be whole, and when the people for whom we pray open themselves to the Spirit, we trust some kind of healing will take place; (2) God, not we, sets the healing agenda, and we may not know what healing will look like in a given case; (3) our first task is to discern what to pray for and how to pray.

17. *Does a person need a special gift of healing in order to pray effectively for healing?*

The apostle Paul names gifts of healing among the spiritual gifts given to the church for the common good (1 Cor. 12:9). In the church today, there do seem to be people with special gifts—whether we think of them as talents, sensitivities, or spiritual gifts—in healing prayer. Such people should be encouraged to discover, own, and cultivate their gifts. It is important, of course, for these gifts to be confirmed within the community of faith.

Most of us, however, do not have extraordinary gifts of healing, but we do have a role in healing prayer. Francis MacNutt has said that healing is a little like music. Although we are not all a Mozart, we can all play an instrument and improve with practice!

The gift of healing is not a private possession, in any case. As Jesus sent forth his disciples to preach and heal and cast out demons, not designating specialists but giving the tasks to all, so churches today are called and gifted to become healing communities. *The gift of healing is given to the whole body of Christ, to be exercised by all the members of the body.* What this means practically is that each member of the faith community should be helped to learn to pray in ways that have personal integrity within the community. For some, this may be nothing more dramatic than silently praying for others at home or in the church pew; for others it may mean joining a prayer circle or a healing team that visits the sick. What is important is that we see the church as a healing community and begin to contribute to that community.[15]

## *Conclusion*

We have worked through a long and daunting list of questions. Even so, we may not have touched upon your personal, most urgent concerns. Questions about healing prayer, whatever they may be, are important and valid. Although we cannot hope to have answered these questions fully here, you now have a starting point for further reflection. Continue questioning to deepen and enrich your process of exploring healing prayer.

## CHAPTER THREE

# Praying for the Person God Is Calling Me to Be

Lois is committed to a journey of healing. For years, she has prayed daily that God will "grow" her, and indeed she has grown enormously. She has come to expect that God's healing grace will beckon her forward even when circumstances are difficult.

Recently, Lois's alcoholic father died after a long illness. She had lovingly looked after him for several years until the end. Early in his illness, Lois's rage toward her father bubbled to the surface. She realized she was furious that he had not been much of a father to begin with, and as he grew older his addiction claimed more and more of his life. As her anger surged, she expressed it in her journal, painted it, and beat up pillows. She sobbed and yelled her anger to her therapist. Although she chose not to explode at her dying father directly, she felt her anger deeply and allowed its expression.

Then one day she imagined Jesus asking that her anger be given to him. It seemed to her that she was carrying all her anger from childhood gathered up in a housepainter's drop cloth. In her prayerful imagination she handed the large bundle to Jesus, who accepted it and threw it away. She felt freer and lighter than she had in months, truly rid of the anger that had poisoned her life.

Some time after this, she "heard" as she prayed that she should tell her father that she loved him. Words of love had rarely been uttered as Lois was growing up, and voicing them was not easy for her as an adult. She tried to get the words out, but they seemed stuck in her throat. She asked God to help her do this difficult thing, but nothing happened right away.

A few weeks later Lois's cat was hit by a car. Holding her mortally wounded pet, Lois sank down on the floor and sobbed while her father continued to focus on the television. Suddenly it "clicked" that her inconsolable weeping, ignored by her father, epitomized her childhood. Just as suddenly she felt the courage for which she had prayed. Newly empowered, she blurted out, "Pop, you see how much I'm crying now? Well, when you die I'm going to cry even harder." Then the words she had been trying to say for so long just came tumbling out. "I love you, Pop." He did not respond, but she knew he heard. After that it was easier to say "Daddy, I love you."

As she repeated the loving words day after day, her own capacity to love and forgive grew rapidly. She found herself tenderly loving and forgiving this old man who had hurt her so deeply as a child and who, even now, could not return her caring words and actions. She was able to give up her need to have him love her in a particular way, and she could accept him just as he was. In the process she grew to be a little bit more like Jesus. More at peace, more joyful, and less physically tense, she was able to say good-bye when her father died, and she freely cried out her grief.

A few months after her father's death, Lois felt a renewed call to work with persons who are HIV positive or those who have AIDS. Her experience with her father was being turned into a gift to work with others who were dying. Lois was healed, not in the sense of arriving somehow at a state of perfect health, but in the sense of being gently led and accompanied on a healing journey toward wholeness in mind, body, emotions, and spirit.

Some people find it easier to pray for others than for themselves. However, the more we pray for the brokenness and pain of other people, the more we are made aware of our own need for healing. With growing sensitivity, we will see ourselves in many of the people for whom we pray. We know we are indeed wounded healers. If we are open, we will sense God's invitation to grow toward wholeness, just as Lois did.

Lois's story illustrates many of the points outlined in the definition of Christian healing in chapter 1. Following is a review of the key phrases.

## God's Desire for Human Wholeness

God desires our health, our wholeness of body, mind, and spirit. This bold affirmation rests on the knowledge and experience of God in the life of Israel and the church. God was revealed to Israel as "the LORD, who heals you" (Exod. 15:26), whose deepest and most consistent desire was to redeem, bless, and restore God's people. God's covenant relationship with Israel was a call to personal and social wholeness, to shalom. That God desires our wholeness is most clearly seen in the words and deeds of Jesus. Jesus spoke of God as the loving parent who will "give good things to those who ask" (Matt. 7:11). With piercing simplicity, Jesus thus provided a window into the compassionate heart of God. In his deeds of healing Jesus embodied that same compassion, showing by his own actions that God desires people to be well and whole.

Let us be honest: it is bold to affirm that God desires our wholeness, because human experience is so often to the contrary. Frequently God's desire for wholeness is frustrated. As we saw in chapter 2, much human suffering arises from the free operation of creation, resulting in what is called natural evil, and from the free will of humans, often resulting in what is called moral evil, or sin. Though such factors often do frustrate God's desire for wholeness, they do not refute what God's desire is. Christians affirm that the ultimate fulfillment of God's desire lies in the final triumph of God over every enemy in the realm of God, what Paul spoke of as "the freedom of the glory of the children of God" (Rom. 8:21).

In the here and now we can count on this: that whenever we open ourselves to the activity of the Holy Spirit, some kind of healing takes place. Indeed, God invites us to ask for what we need just as a child would ask a parent. Even when our lives are filled with suffering or wracked with agonizing questions, we can cling to the faith that God is with us, somehow always offering new life and healing. Not all healing will be physical, of course; often healing comes in emotional and spiritual realms where God's love is able to overcome every obstacle.

## Discerning Who God Is Calling Me to Be

God not only yearns for our wholeness but is also actively involved in our growth. The wholeness offered to each person is unique and particular, rooted in God's will for each person. Each person's state of "health" is different, and for each one, healing will follow a different course. One person who prays for physical healing is restored instantly, even as he or she prays. For another, physical healing takes longer. Often the healing process takes a person into realms of emotional and spiritual healing before physical healing occurs. Sometimes physical healing is not given at all, but the person is healed in ways that make the physical condition a gift.

In addition, each person has a different personality and life history. Whether you are fiery and energetic or serene and laid-back, whether you have lived a tragic life or one of relative ease and happiness, God molds this material into your particular call to wholeness. Like a tree growing around a boulder, we are invited to grow around our own obstacles. Furthermore, the specifics of the way God heals you will change over the course of your life. The healing agenda for a lonely teenager is different from that of a busy forty-two-year-old, and still different for a person of great age preparing for death.[1]

If we view healing as a process unique for each person, the following implications become evident:

1. When we speak of healing, we do not necessarily mean the restoration of perfect health, but moving toward God's perfect will for us at each stage of our lives.

2. Healing prayer is not just for the times when we are sick or troubled, but is for a lifetime, process of growth and maturation into the person God created us to be.

3. God's healing is not some sort of divine zap, which comes from outside. Rather it is the result of God's active engagement in and with every part of our being.

4. Christian healing prayer is a process of discovering and praying for whatever the Holy Spirit is bringing to birth in us. It is the surrender to God's continuing creation in us.

## *Discernment*

The process of discovering God's will is called discernment. While discernment is at the heart of healing prayer, and indeed is essential to any serious attempt to live a Christian life, the term has not been familiar to many Protestant Christians. It has, however, been a part of the church's wisdom throughout the ages. One of the richest sources of wisdom about discernment is the sixteenth century classic *The Spiritual Exercises* by Saint Ignatius of Loyola.[2]

Saint Ignatius would be quite familiar with the way spiritual directors of our own time seek to assist serious Christians with discernment. Although the process of discernment and the practice of spiritual direction itself have traditionally been gifts of the Roman Catholic church, increasingly Protestants are among those learning how to discern God's continuing invitation.

Some may mistakenly think of spiritual discernment as having absolutely certain knowledge of God's will in a specific situation. They wonder how anyone can be "that sure" and may be turned off by Christians who punctuate every sentence with "God told me. . . ." Or they may feel that, while some very saintly people know God's specific will, ordinary people probably can know God's will only in a general way. Thus, they feel the best they can do is to figure out a general direction based on the Bible and the wisdom of the church and then add to that their own common sense.

In fact, appeals to Scripture, tradition, and reason are surely part of any responsible discernment process. We test the validity of what we perceive by asking ourselves: *Does this sound like the God of the Bible? Does it reflect the best thinking of the church? Does it make sense?*[3]

But there is more to discernment than inference. *Discernment is rooted in the belief that God seeks to be in personal relationship with each of us.*

In faith we believe that God speaks to us personally about our particular lives.

How does this happen in the life of a Christian? It happens through inviting God to speak and then listening—not for audible sounds from heaven, but for the still, small voice that speaks through what is going on around us and inside us.

God speaks in many different ways, and grace gives us the eyes to see and the ears to hear. For example, God may speak through pictures that form in our mind as we pray, or in ideas that seem to float into our awareness. We may suddenly remember a verse from scripture, a hymn text, or something that happened long ago. Or, God may speak through dreams, or events, or in words spoken by a friend.[4] The important thing is to pray for the grace to know God's voice, to test it a bit, and then to act in faith on the discernment given, trusting that God will correct us if we have not heard quite clearly.

Discernment, then, is not looking for "skywriting," God's telling us exactly what we need to know. It very seldom happens that way. Rather, in discerning we pray for grace that we might enter into a lively and dynamic awareness of what God is communicating to us in the changing circumstances of our lives.[5]

## Steps in a Discernment Process

The idea of spiritual discernment may seem strange and esoteric to those unfamiliar with the practice. In fact it is not hard to begin to practice the basic steps of a simple discernment process. Here is a brief description of steps in discernment for healing prayer. Imagine that you are seeking to discern how God desires to move in your life now, how God wants to heal you.

1. Tell God how you feel, as honestly as you can. Do not get pious about this. Take a lesson from the Psalms. If you feel like choking someone with your bare hands, say so. If you doubt that God is paying attention, say that too. If you are depressed, confused, worried, sick of being sick, admit it. This step is very important, one often skipped by Christians who want to keep everything nice.

2. Invite God into all of your brokenness. Ask God to heal you and to show you what to pray for.

3. Then stop talking—even in your head—and simply sit in God's presence, with the expectation that God will work in some way. Allow some time for this, say fifteen to twenty minutes.

4. Pay attention to what happens in the silence: What images, thoughts, and memories arise? What physical sensations? What desires? What emerges as an action you should take?

5. You might want to imagine Jesus with you. What does he say to you? What does he do? (This way of praying, called "faith imagination," will be discussed later in this chapter).

6. It may be helpful to jot down briefly whatever impressions come to you as you pray.

7. You may immediately see a pattern in your perceptions that suggests a direction for prayer. If so, act on this discernment by praying along the lines suggested.

8. Do not be discouraged if nothing much seems to happen. Keep asking, and remember that God speaks in many ways. Be open to God's voice and action in books you read, phone calls you receive, events in your life, and so on. Remember how powerfully God acted in the death of Lois's cat as Lois prayed that she could say to her father, "I love you."

9. Asking other Christians to assist you in your discernment process can be tremenduously helpful and can protect you from distortion.

10. Trust that if your discernment is off the mark, the Holy Spirit will somehow correct you. Simply remain as open as possible and act in faith on whatever discernment you receive.

11. If your discernment process truly draws a blank, of course you can still pray. You might say something like, "Lord, I don't know how you want to heal me, but I know you are a God of love and compassion. Please heal me in the way that is best for me."

Here is a simple situation that illustrates discernment. Imagine that you pray about having "the blahs." Nothing seems exciting or interesting, and you feel tired all the time, even though on the surface things seem to be going well. As you wait for God to work, you see in your mind the face of a person who hurt you. You remember what the person did and how you reacted. *Trust that this memory came up at this time for a reason and that it is somehow related to the issue at hand.* After all, you asked God to work in you! So, in response to your discernment, shift your focus from your lack of energy to the image of the one who hurt you. Ask God to help you release your anger and forgive the person. Continue to ask God for discernment about the steps you need to take in this process.

If you are praying about the blahs and you get the notion to have a physical examination, do it. Trust enough to act on whatever direction you are given if your action is reasonable and consistent with the God of the Bible.

Tilda reports the following dream after asking for discernment about her feeling the blahs:

A friend who is a fine classical musician walked up to me and with great seriousness gazed into my eyes for several minutes. She did not smile or blink, and I had the sense that something important was about to happen. Then gravely she asked me a question: "Tilda, what if 'Inky Dinky Parlez Vous' was really written by Bach?" After a solemn pause, she broke into delighted peals of laughter. I woke up laughing myself and sensing that God had indeed answered my prayer. It seemed clear that I needed to lighten up, to see the humor even in "serious" things, to have fun, to be silly at times. As I prayed for the grace to do this, over the next few weeks the plodding, gray fatigue that I had been experiencing gradually melted away.

## Pursuing the Call to Wholeness

Recall part of our definition of Christian healing: "Because the Holy Spirit is continually at work in each of us, pushing us toward wholeness, the process of healing is like removing sticks and leaves from a stream until the water runs clear. If we simply get out of the way of the Lord's work in us, we can trust that we are being led to the particular kind of wholeness God wills for us."

It sounds simple, doesn't it? All we have to do is get out of the way of God's work in us and some kind of healing will flow. Yet we know it is not so simple. Taking the sticks and leaves away may be painful. With them gone we may feel afraid or uncomfortable. Not by chance did Jesus ask the man waiting to be healed by the pool of Siloam, "Do you want to be made well?" (John 5:6). Like that man, many of us may find it hard to give up a way of life that feels familiar even though painful. We hang onto our suffering, often clutching painful memories, resentments, or guilt as though they were treasures.[6] Even physical suffering may have a payoff.

When Janet has the flu for a few days, mostly she does not enjoy being sick; she cannot wait to feel better. But while she is sick, her family brings her tea and toast in bed. They screen her phone calls and make things as easy as possible for her. She has to admit that some nice perks accompany being sick.

Such responses can play out in a major illness on a large scale. Not that everyone with a major physical illness is actually a sneaky malingerer who enjoys being the center of attention. Far from it! But with suffering comes a healthy drive to make life more tolerable for ourselves. Sometimes we adapt so well to a life of illness and pain that we find it hard to let go of our adaptations when the time comes to be well.

Major illnesses have been known to cement a faltering relationship or to provide the perfect reason for not engaging in a demanding task.[7] This can be true of emotional and spiritual pain as well. Someone once asked: "Who will I be if I give up my depression? I can't imagine being me and not being depressed. It's who I am."

One way to "clear the stream" is to ask ourselves and God whether we experience any payoff in our suffering. Are we holding on to something self-defeating, even a little? Often the beginning of healing means surrendering false securities to God with a prayer that God will fill the function they had in our lives. Instead of depending on our brokenness to shield us, we might pray that God heal a faltering relationship, that God direct and give courage for the demanding task, that God teach us who we are in our deepest selves. The decision to trust God in this way often opens wide the door to further healing.

We can clear the stream for God's work in us in other ways. We can allow "bad" feelings to surface as we pray. Honestly recognizing our anger, our lust, our doubts, and so on opens us to our brokenness, where God works. We can grow in willingness to surrender plans, habits of behavior and thought, or an insistence that things happen in a certain way. We can be willing to risk scary or difficult actions, such as asking someone for forgiveness. We can notice our rigidities and ask God that they be softened. If we catch ourselves saying such things as, "I will never forget what he did to me," we can be willing to give up such ideas about how things have to be. We can pray to become more supple, submitting all that we are to the loving touch of the Holy Spirit.

Although the healing process integrally involves our emotions, sometimes our emotions lag behind, and our will must lead the way. If we have been deeply hurt, we may not be able to change our feelings of shame, fear, or anger toward the one who hurt us. However, we can fully acknowledge these feelings, express them somehow in all their depth, and then with our will ask Jesus to change our heart. God seems to honor this request with an outpouring of healing grace. Remember that Lois could not change her anger toward her father by herself, but by surrendering it to God she was deeply healed. Sometimes it seems that we have to go on sheer willpower for a time, but eventually God heals us when we give all things over into God's hands.

As we continue to clear our stream of obstacles to wholeness, it is important to remember the wonderfully intricate interconnectedness of the physical, emotional, spiritual, and mental dimensions of the human person. We can trust God to bring to the surface whatever needs to be healed most in us, because we know that God wants to "grow" us. And we can trust that, as we work with one area of our lives, God cares for the rest.

## Issues in Physical Healing

Many people who are beginning to pray for healing seem naturally to focus first on physical healing. Physical healing has long been the province of television healers, and, for some, physical healing is the only "real" healing. Even those of us who have a holistic view sometimes feel tempted to emphasize physical healing over healing in other areas. Yet often the physical dimension is the last to be touched by deep healing. And sometimes physical healing does not occur at all.

On the other hand, we have experienced many astonishing physical healings. Once Tilda prayed for a woman who had severe bursitis and was in great pain. Surgery was scheduled for the following week. The pain and the swelling vanished as they prayed together, and the woman has had no trouble since. As a matter of course, when Tilda leads a workshop to introduce the healing ministry, she often asks whether anyone has a minor physical ailment such as a headache or a cold. When the group prays for these small physical problems, the person is almost always healed or greatly improved immediately. This experience helps build a group's faith in God's response to healing prayer.

It is not clear why small physical ailments seem more readily healed than larger ones. After all, God has no more difficulty healing cancer than the flu. Nor is it easy to explain why someone might experience deep healing in her emotions and spirit, and yet improve only a little physically. Experience suggests that seldom is someone healed physically and not touched in emotions or spirit. Perhaps the faith of those who pray is a factor here. All of this says to us that God, working through our limitations and gifts, heals. If we are in physical distress, by all means we pray with trust for physical healing, unless our discernment is telling us otherwise.

It may be important to pray with persistence. Sometimes it seems that physical healing happens only after praying for a period of time, say an hour or two, or weekly over many months. Francis MacNutt calls this "soaking prayer," a process in which we direct our attention to a need for healing, and then rest in God's presence, inviting God to work through us.[8] In soaking prayer, we might sing hymns softly or just slip into wordless silence. When we pray in this way, God seems to irradiate the person prayed for with love.

One woman who received soaking prayer was losing the function of her kidneys and was told she had at most two years to live. She was prayed for in a group once a month for sixteen months for about ten to fifteen minutes at a time. The prayer sessions were taped, and she listened to the tapes daily at home. Three years later, she had more kidney function each time she was tested. Her doctors were mystified. At this writing, a decade later, she is still alive and active in volunteer ministry.

## *Issues in Emotional Healing*

All of us have had experiences that hurt us and have stunted our emotional or spiritual growth. We may have had parents who belittled us or even physically abused us. We might have experienced tragedy or violence or been the victims of societal prejudice and hatred. Because of such experiences we may carry deep scars of sorrow, an abiding mistrust of the world, or emotional numbness. Probably each of us can identify a need for healing in our emotions.

*Faith imagination.* One of the most effective ways to pray for emotional healing is through a process called "faith imagination."[9] In this process, using our natural, human capacity for imaginative thought, we invite Jesus to join us in the place where we hurt. This may mean going back in time with Jesus to a painful memory and imaginatively reliving it with Jesus present. Or it might mean simply imagining Jesus in the room with us as we pray.

In her work with individuals, Tilda often witnesses Jesus responding to this invitation by working through the imagination to love someone back to wholeness. Sometimes, when a painful childhood scene is being relived, Jesus holds and comforts an adult who, for that moment, is a frightened child. Or he may act to protect her from those who hurt her, putting himself between the "child" and an adult abuser and receiving the abuse into his own body. This usually brings deep healing for the sufferer. Sometimes Jesus weeps, or in other instances may involve the "child" in hilarious play. Often he speaks words that transform the person; sometimes just his presence makes all the difference. It is deeply moving to witness the myriad ways Jesus enters into the lives of hurting people through their imaginations to bring exactly the kind of experience that will be healing for them. People who were considered hopeless cases in psychotherapy have been marvelously healed. Jesus does indeed enter into our deepest pain and there "loves, transforms, forgives, redeems, resurrects, and heals."

Human imagination is a wonderfully complex capacity, so it is important to note that people vary greatly in the form their imagination takes. Some are oriented toward the visual and tend to imagine in pictures. Others never see pictures but imagine with hearing or bodily sensations. Still others imagine with cognitive ideas that prompt their emotions and memories. Most employ a mixture of these modalities, but will prefer one over the others. Accept the way in which you imagine, and allow God to communicate with you in whatever way God may choose.

Praying with faith imagination is not difficult, but it can be intense. It is profoundly involving and demands as much honesty and openness as we can muster. After praying for guidance, the first step is, as much as possible, to experience—not just think about—what needs to be healed. This could mean allowing ourselves to feel "unacceptable" emotions, or face a difficult question head-on, or return to a painful memory.

Suppose a memory of an accident presents itself for healing. In faith imagination we go back to our memory of the accident, staying with it until the memory is as vivid and nuanced as possible. If emotions surface, we welcome them and let them be. Then we invite Jesus—or another symbol of God—to enter our memory of the accident: "Lord, please be with me in this accident. Show me how you were there when it happened. Please show me what you want to do now."

The next step is just to pay imaginative attention to what happens next. Let Jesus appear in your mind's eye or speak into your mind's ear. Let your body experience his presence. What does Jesus do? How does he respond to you? What does he say or give you to know? In a memory of an accident, we might see Jesus touching those who were hurt or taking someone who died to a new heavenly life. Or we might hear him speak words of comfort.

God's response in faith imagination prayer often will seem tailor-made for the needs of the person praying. A minister, praying with faith imagination about an accident that claimed the life of his mother when he was seven, saw Jesus hand him his alb and stole. Jesus then told him to use the words of a funeral service to commit his mother to God's care. As the minister did this, he was finally able to say good-bye and to release his anger over her death. Later he said that the experience had a curious personal "rightness" about it for him.

Take enough time for the experience to play out and conclude by itself. It is important that anyone assisting the person praying not push or try to make something happen. The best tactic for supporting another in faith imagination is to watch and pray, for the most part silently! Finally, thank God for what happened and ask to be enabled to take it in, allowing it to change you.

As you try faith imagination prayer, you may find yourself asking, "Am I making all this up?" People naturally wonder whether this kind of prayer means simply dreaming a rosy picture made of fantasy and wishes, with a little religion thrown in. It is understandable to wonder whether this is prayer at all, or only an attempt to manipulate God.

Obviously, it is possible to distort almost any process, including faith imagination. Even at best, our experience and expectations color all our perceptions. But God is able to get around our limitations.

Furthermore, it is striking how often the quality of the response from Jesus is not in the emotional repertoire of the one praying. A deeply depressed individual cannot usually dredge up a heartfelt message of hope, no matter how great the effort. One who is terrified cannot find a way to feel safe just by thinking about it. Often a quality of "otherness" and surprise touches us through the action of God when we pray in this way.

The most compelling evidence that God is indeed at work in faith imagination is simply that people are healed. Pain that has been present for years may vanish or greatly diminish, and the healing seems to take deep root in the person. Tilda worked with a woman who had been sexually abused by her father many times. The woman's picture of herself as a child was "a dirty kid, ashamed of myself, in a dirty dress with yucky stuff all over me." In faith imagination prayer, the woman saw Jesus stride into her childhood bedroom. He lifted her off the bed and took her outside to a river. There he washed her, gently and respectfully. Then Jesus gave her a new, pretty dress and helped her put it on. Later on, she reflected that the washing in the river was very similar to baptism, raising her to new life. But right then, she just felt marvelously clean. The prayer image ended with Jesus taking her to buy an ice cream cone. A year later, she continued to feel deeply cleansed by this experience.

## *Issues in Spiritual Healing*

As we experience God's healing physically or emotionally, we can be confident that God is touching our spirit as well. Just to believe that God is at work in us is in itself a joyful, marvelous thing. Conversely, physical or emotional pain has a spiritual component. It follows that the more we welcome God's activity into every level of our being, the more we will be spiritually whole.

Spiritual healing takes many forms. Often it is simply a matter of being enabled to give up our anxiety or worry in order to trust that God is at work. We may be given the grace to love and forgive someone whom we see as unlovable. As we feel God's love pouring over us, we may come to love ourselves more deeply, despite our brokenness.

One familiar form of spiritual healing is God's forgiveness of sin. Most churches proclaim God's mercy each Sunday during community worship, in the belief that God puts the past behind us and sets us on the path of new life. At the center of our faith is the belief that when we ask for forgiveness and are truly sorry, God always answers such prayer with a Yes. Consequently, genuine guilt can be addressed very easily by Christians. We simply ask for forgiveness and know that it is given. If we willingly accept God's forgiveness of all the sin of our life, we know profound healing. For many, such confession and forgiveness opens the door into the Christian life.

However, many accept the idea of God's forgiveness but are not able to allow this forgiveness to penetrate their hearts. In other words, they cannot forgive themselves. People in this state may need emotional healing through faith imagination prayer, or may need to "soak" in God's love over a period of time before God's forgiveness can cleanse them. Or, they may need to hear personally in a confidential setting that God has forgiven them.

Finally, there is a type of spiritual healing called deliverance. In deliverance prayer, we lay claim to the victory of Jesus over evil, commanding it in his name to leave. Deliverance prayer is grounded in the bold Easter faith that Jesus Christ, as victor over the forces of evil (Satan), endows Christians with the authority to address these forces in his name.

Jesus occasionally healed by commanding the forces of evil to depart and commissioned his disciples to do the same. Paul and his followers also roundly affirmed Jesus' power over the forces of evil.[10] Today, experienced ministers of healing still affirm that demonic forces flee upon command in the name of Jesus Christ.

It is important to understand that deliverance prayer is called for only when evil seems to hold a person in bondage, manifesting itself in different degrees of severity. In addition, the evil forces usually interact in a complex way with the sufferer's brokenness and particular personal history. Although deliverance prayer is obviously not appropriate for everyone, it can be crucial to those who truly need it. Through deliverance, we can bear witness to the marvelous power of Jesus to bring "release to the captives" (Luke 4:1 8) as we enlist the authority of Jesus over evil. For example, one woman was freed from frequent seizures after deliverance prayer, another from episodes of uncontrollable rage.

Certainly deliverance prayer should not be seen as magic, or an easy answer, or a way simply to get rid of what one does not like about oneself. In these matters we should avoid fascination with the power of evil and keep our hearts at rest in the power of the risen Lord.

A detailed discussion of deliverance prayer takes us far beyond the scope of this book. If you suspect a need for deliverance healing, read further on the subject and use careful discernment.[11] Most important, find someone wise, balanced, and experienced in deliverance to assist you.

## Being a Whole Person

It should be clear by now that whole persons are those on a heal- ing journey. Praying for healing renews and deepens our relation- ship with God. Through healing prayer we discern God's will and sur- render ourselves to God's action. This healing journey teaches us to find the gift that our suffering and brokenness offer to us. It leads us to expect that we will be transformed and that what has been terrible in our lives will be redeemed, even turned into a gift. As one woman put it, "All my worst stuff has become my best stuff."

A final outcome of this journey toward wholeness is to be gifted with joy. Yes, God seems to want to heal us in order to empower us for effective ministry. But more important, God heals because God loves. In the Gospel of John, Jesus describes himself beautifully as the vine and his followers as the branches. Then, perhaps gazing tenderly at his friends, he says, "I have said these things to you so that my joy may be in you, and that your joy may be complete" (John 15:11). As we continue on our own healing journeys, may this joy take root in us.

## The Healing of a Tragedy

The story of Kathleen illustrates much of what we have said about praying for the healing of oneself. Kathleen is an active laywoman, the mother of three grown children, and a person of prayer. This story concerns her son Jay.

Jay had been a little depressed and confused about what he wanted to do as a career, but no one thought he was deeply troubled. In his early twenties, he seemed to be a normal young man. So it was a horrifying shock to Jay's family when he shot himself, leaving his disfigured body to be discovered in his apartment. Full of searing grief, Kathleen's spirit screamed, *Why? Why didn't he come to us? We would have helped him. What did I do wrong? Why didn't I pick up the signals that something was so wrong? What drove him to this? Where was God? Why didn't God stop him?*

Her terrible pain began to express itself physically as tension in Kathleen's neck, jaw, and mouth. Over a period of two years she became more and more tense until her mouth was so tight her speech was seriously affected. Extensive medical tests found no organic or physical explanation.

When Tilda first met her, Kathleen's speech was almost impossible to understand. Her mouth seemed to be frozen into an expression of horror and pain. Sometimes she even looked as if she were still gazing at Jay's mangled body.

She and Tilda worked together, mostly praying with faith imagination. As Kathleen prayed, she would usually sense Jesus standing in front of her. Sometimes he spoke, and his speaking addressed the questions of her heart. Sometimes he was silent but his presence alone comforted her. She often cried to him and felt he was somehow receiving her tears. Once she imagined Jesus wept with her, carrying her grief. Another time she felt the Lord inviting her to scream out her horror. She did this, even though hers was a sedate family and she never remembered screaming before. Gradually her speech improved as she continued to allow the Lord to work in her.

At one point she discerned that she was subtly holding onto her speech impediment. She came to recognize it as a way of holding onto Jay. As long as she could not talk, his memory stayed alive. Soon, she was able to "give" Jay to Jesus to care for, and she visualized Jay walking arm in arm with Jesus. He looked happy and content; in fact, he was almost dancing. She found this image greatly comforting, and her speaking ability took a leap forward.

However, her healing had not yet touched the deepest question of Kathleen's hurting heart. When Jay was alive, he had told her once that he believed in God but "not the same way you do, Ma." The memory of this conversation made Kathleen terribly afraid that Jay had not gone to heaven, because she assumed that he might not have believed in Jesus. Besides that, she wondered what God did about people who committed suicide. Would Jay be punished somehow? Would God really punish someone as upset as Jay must have been? She could hardly bear to think about it.

After agonizing over these questions for months, Kathleen finally brought them to Jesus in a faith imagination prayer. In a marvelous outpouring of grace, she heard Jesus say to her, "Jay believed in God, so Jay also believed in me." She burst into tears, as months of tension and fear drained away. This answer was a powerful salve for her pain, and soon many other things began falling into place for her. Questions about the Trinity that had long troubled her, doubts about God's mercy and love, worry about Jay's soul all seemed to be met in Jesus' simple answer. Kathleen looks back on this graced moment as one of the high points of her spiritual life.

Today Kathleen has a joyful, vibrant faith in God's love and an unshakable conviction that Jesus stands with her through troubled times. She is more deeply compassionate toward others who are in pain. Although her speech is much improved, she still has a slight speech impediment. "Why?" still echoes faintly. She is still on the journey toward wholeness.

## CHAPTER FOUR

# A Simple Gift: Praying for Another's Healing

A worried woman once brought her month-old daughter to Tilda's healing service to be prayed for. Because the baby's intestines were not fully developed at birth, she could not have a bowel movement without help. The mother had been warned by her pediatrician that the baby would need surgery if her intestines did not mature quickly. Our few moments of discernment suggested that God wanted us to pray for the physical healing of this child. We put our hands on the baby while the mother prayed an unrefined, heartfelt prayer: "O Lord, I love my baby! Please give us a poo-poo in this diaper." About a minute after beginning to pray, our prayer group heard the loveliest sound and smelled the most wonderful stink imaginable from the baby's bottom. The diaper was filled by the baby on her own for the first time, a concrete and beautiful sign that God was surely at work.

The baby is now almost ten years old. She never had surgery because ever since the time of the prayer, her intestines have worked just fine.

## A Simple Gift

In the New Testament we read many stories of people bringing loved ones to Jesus for healing or coming to Jesus on behalf of others. Recall the paralytic lowered through the roof by four resourceful friends (Mark 2:1-12) or the epileptic boy brought to Jesus by his distraught father (Mark 9:14-29). Think of Jairus going to Jesus on behalf of his daughter (Mark 5:21-24, 35-43) or the centurion who approached Jesus because his servant was paralyzed (Matt. 8:5-13). In the Gospels, Jesus always responds to these requests by healing the person.

In this chapter we will explore more deeply what is involved in "bringing our loved ones to Jesus." We know healing prayer to be a simple gift, a profoundly moving way in which God shows love for us. God gives the gift of healing to the church, which invites, indeed calls, all of us to pray for the healing of others.[1]

Brother Roger, the prior of the Taizé ecumenical monastic community in France, once said that of all people, small children should be the ones who pray for healing. Then, when healing takes place, there can be no mistaking that God is at work, not a powerful, influential leader. Ideally, when we as adults pray for healing, we become like small, trusting children—asking for what we want, telling our Parent where it hurts, and trusting the Parent to take care of it.

## Getting Out of the Way

While it is very natural to pray earnestly for our loved ones in need, we can learn ways to channel our natural compassion that will make for more effective praying. Here are some ways to help get ourselves out of the way so that the Lord can work in and through us.

It is important to let go of rules and techniques, so God will have room to work. Much of the spiritual preparation for healing prayer has to do with knowing our helplessness and emptiness on the one hand, and God's overflowing love and mercy on the other. Prayer for healing means inviting God to work in the person in God's own way.

Certain temptations, however, threaten to place us in the way of God's action.

*The temptation to be in control.* We may be tempted to come to God as grown-ups who "know best," who want to appear competent, who have a good theory or theology, who perhaps even have special skills in a helping profession. The temptation to be in control is the theme underlying all the other temptations mentioned below.

*The temptation to insist on a formula.* We may come to God armed with a rigid system of rules for healing prayer. Sometimes when prayers for healing are answered, we expect God to work in the same way the next time. Perhaps we have been led to pray in a particular manner, even two or three times. Then it is tempting to think that we have the healing process all figured out. We imagine we know how God will act in a particular instance. What began as a response to God's unique work with individuals becomes a pattern we try to impose on everybody. Of course, God will not be put into a little box—or a big one!

*The temptation to look good.* This temptation entices us to pray for the healing of others in a way that will make us look holy or satisfy our need to be powerful. People tend to put healers on a pedestal, and it is easy to oblige them. Newcomers to healing prayer may not be tempted in this way, but those with experience in healing prayer will face the temptation to arrogance sooner or later.

If we find we are eager for admiration and gratitude, if we begin to love how everyone asks us for help, if we start to see ourselves as different and holier than others, it is time to confess the sin of arrogance and pride. We pray for grace to see the truth: that we are ourselves wounded healers, simply channels God sometimes uses.[2]

One way to head off hero worship before it starts is to pray with a partner or prayer team. When healing occurs, it is more likely that God, rather than the healer, will receive the credit. Furthermore, team members can helpfully watch for signs of pride in each other. Of course we can certainly pray alone for someone and we should. But churches with healing ministries might consider adopting a healing team approach, so that no one is identified as the principal healer. A healing team also conveys the message that healing prayer is a ministry given to the church as a whole and not just to a few unusually gifted people.[3]

*The temptation to judge.* Another temptation persuades us to let our personal judgments and brokenness crowd out God's work. Once Tilda was asked to pray for a man who had strong urges toward voyeurism. He had the urge to peek through windows to watch women as they undressed. He had actually done this a few times and was making heroic efforts to control his compulsive behavior. He felt terribly guilty for having these urges and desperately wanted to be healed. He came for help, humbly hoping to be freed.

Tilda could not, however, see him as a struggling man whom God loved in his brokenness. All she was aware of was the loud judgment in her own mind: "How awful! Another man using women to get his kicks! How could he?" Obviously, Tilda was in no state to pray for this man, and not much happened during their time together.

It was only later that Tilda remembered how, as a child, she was very curious about how people's bodies looked and had done some peeking of her own when she was seven or eight. She realized that she had retained her own childish guilt and that it had prevented her from loving this man.

This story teaches an important lesson. If we are turned off, judgmental, scared, disgusted, or shocked, we probably have work to do ourselves. Something in us needs to be healed. In such a case, we would be well advised to let someone else pray for the other person until we work out our own issues. Remember, we all are wounded healers.

*The temptation to trust our own skills or faith, rather than God.* In chapter 2 we examined the relation of faith to healing. When we put trust in the strength of our faith, or imagine that faith somehow manufactures healing, we simply betray our need for control. Although God surely does use whatever gifts we have, we dare not trust solely in our own intuition or learned skills. No matter how faith-filled we are, no matter what our skills and gifts, it is God who heals. We put our trust in God, not in ourselves.

Often the professional person with many healing skills has the most trouble praying in simple trust that God is already at work in both the person who has sought prayers and in the healer, making up for what is lacking in faith or skills. A helpful approach for such a professional is to seek counsel with a trusted friend or spiritual director, inviting him or her to point out signs of putting faith in self rather than in God.

*The temptation to predict how God will work.* It may momentarily give hope to say to a sufferer, "I know that God will take away your cancer." But unless those praying for another's healing are absolutely certain through extraordinary discernment, such a statement is highly irresponsible. It would be much more faithful to say, "I don't know just how God will answer us, but I do know that God loves you and wants your wholeness. Let's invite God to use our prayers to do whatever God wants."

*The temptation to impose our agenda for healing.* It is enormously tempting to pray for healing while insisting on our agenda for the person prayed for. This does not mean that we should pray only in vague generalities. It does mean that we trust that God loves this person even more than we do and that God knows what is best better than we do. It is crucial to pray for specifics only after we have discerned what God wants to do for the person.

A healing team of which Tilda was a part learned this in a process that was both painful and deeply moving. Jeff, a twenty-one-year-old college student and a member of the track team, found out that he had amyotrophic lateral sclerosis (ALS), also called Lou Gehrig's disease. This terrible disease attacks muscles, including the heart and lungs, causing them to disintegrate. When Jeff first heard that he had about two years to live, he was furiously angry. He railed. He swore. He yelled. He cried. He could not stand to see anyone who was healthy or happy. He was going to die and he was certain no one cared, not even his parents.

When our prayer team began to pray for Jeff, we prayed earnestly that he would be healed of ALS, that he would go back to school and run again. We prayed that he would not die. Sharing Jeff's feeling that death at such a young age was unfair and awful, we prayed with our own agenda. We yearned somehow to magically control what was happening to him.

We all liked Jeff a lot. It was very painful to see that each time he came for prayer he had less and less control of his muscles. His disease was progressing fast. The healing team was bewildered and upset. Yet God was powerfully at work. God met Jeff in all of his fear, confusion, and despair and started to change things for him. Through our prayers Jeff felt prompted to deal with his troubled relationship with his parents. As he began to face their very real rejection of him, he expressed his rage—and then let it flow away. After letting go of his anger, he was able to see them clearly as two broken people who had loved him the best way they could. Soon he forgave them and came to appreciate them for the first time in his life.

He also admitted that he had caused pain to a number of women friends. He would drop them after a few months of romantic interest after making promises to them that he had known he would not keep. He started writing to the women, ask-ing their forgiveness. Most of them forgave and supported him during his dying process. As these personal matters began to clear up in his life, Jeff began to feel better, despite the progressing disease.

Gradually the prayer group began to see that God was healing something within Jeff that we had never considered. It was hard for us to let go of our agenda for him, but the more we were able to surrender, the more Jeff seemed to benefit from our prayers.

As Jeff invited Jesus into his life more and more, his spiritual life deepened into radiance. He began to be so certain of God's love that he would say to people, "I know I'm dying, but I wouldn't exchange my life for anyone else's in the world. I know I'm dying, but I've been healed. I know I'm dying, but if I didn't have this illness, I would never have had this joy." And, indeed, it was obvious that Jeff was living in profound joy.

About a year before he died, Jeff began to be unafraid of dying; in fact he was almost eager for it, looking forward to death as an adventure. He and a friend made a video of his last months, in which he tried to relate the message that even death for a Christian is finally not a tragedy. For Jeff, death was his healing, setting him free from pain and bondage and ushering him into new life.

Jeff deeply touched all of us who knew him. We had not wanted his kind of healing in the beginning. We found it hard to give up our agenda and were terribly saddened by his death. But clearly Jeff had been deeply healed, and it seemed that God had used our prayers.

This discussion of temptations and pitfalls might suggest that healing prayer is only for the saintly. Nothing could be further from the truth! Knowing that it is God who heals should give us the courage to pray for healing, even if we are not saints or completely whole ourselves. Seeking discernment before we pray is a concrete way to put our faith in God, not in ourselves.

## Before We Pray for Healing: The Discernment Process

The process of discernment is as important in our prayers for others as it is in praying for ourselves. The following presents an outline of a simple discernment process such as we discussed in the previous chapter, now focused on praying for another.

1. Invite God to use you as a channel of healing and to continue to give you whatever faith, discernment, and love is necessary to help the person you are praying for.

2. Ask God to melt away anything in you that might get in the way: your need for power, your hang-ups or judgment, your brokenness, or your desire to cling to your own agenda. Know that God is able to use you despite these things.

3. Feel your love and compassion for the person. Sometimes this is even more important than faith. Your own love for the person will probably carry with it your human desire for the person. Your instinct may be to say, for example, "I want this person to be healed, physically."

4. Speak your desire to God as honestly and plainly as you can. Put your agenda in God's hands.

5. Then, in silence, ask God how you should pray. Allow your agenda to be changed. Listen for the way God might want to heal this person. Remember, even if a person is eventually healed physically, some other kind of healing may emerge first, for example, the release of anger.

6. After inviting God to shape your agenda, trust that God will communicate with you in some way. Pay attention to mental images, words that form in your heart, physical sensations, hunches, intuitions, verses of Scripture that come to mind, and the like. You might try to pray with faith imagination, seeing Jesus with the person. Remember, God speaks in many ways. It may be easier to trust what you discern when praying with one or more persons rather than alone.

7. Once you sense God speaking in some way, ask yourself, "Does this seem consistent with the character of Jesus?" "Does it sound like the God of the Bible?" "Is it consistent with the best we know of theology and psychology?" "Does it echo the wisdom of the church?" For example, discernment that suggests God is using illness and pain to punish someone for his or her sins is very questionable indeed, because it does not meet the criteria of love and compassion.

8. Proceed with your prayer, humbly using whatever discernment you were given. Act in faith, holding open the possibility that

your discernment is incomplete or even inaccurate. Continue discerning each time you pray.

Say, for example, you discern an image of the person for whom you are praying. You "see" the person smiling and healthy, walking briskly through the woods. You might then pray, "Lord, please heal Jane. Restore her to health, that she may walk in joy with you."

Should your discernment consist of hearing the word "rest," your prayer for healing might then be, "God, please help John to rest deeply. Let him completely rest in your presence, so that you renew every cell of his being. Help him to rest his anxieties and his pain in your everlasting arms."

Or, should you feel sadness well up in you as you pray for discernment, you might share this with the one who has come for prayer. Ask whether he or she senses a pool of sadness within. Or you might simply pray, "Lord, if there is some deep sadness in Gary, we ask that you uncover it and enter into it with him. Heal him, so that he may claim the abundant joy you offer." Gary may not have said a word about being sad. He may have come expressing an entirely different need. But you would pray about sadness because you are acting in faith in response to discernment and because you know of the marvelous interconnection of the body, mind, and spirit.

Also you would pray provisionally—"If there is some deep sadness"—because you need always to keep in mind that you may not have discerned accurately. Humble faith is fundamental to healing prayer.

The story of Jim illustrates the important role of discernment in praying for another person. Jim came to a monthly healing service, suffering from ulcers. He had been in treatment for several years, but the pain had worsened. As the healing team laid hands on Jim, he began to cry. One of the persons praying with him sensed these were tears of grief. Upon mentioning this, Jim said that, although his mother had died several years before, he had not until this moment been able to shed one tear of grief. He marveled at how his tears were being released for the first time, as the healing team put their hands on his stomach pain. The team prayed that he continue to cry until all his accumulated grief was released. By the next month, Jim's ulcers had improved. He had cried a lot, and he generally felt much better. As the team placed their hands on his stomach and asked God how to pray, Jim realized that he was still angry at his mother, who had become quite cranky and difficult to live with before she died. This important discernment came from the sufferer, rather than from the prayer team. The prayer this time was that Jim be able to express his anger and then forgive his mother. Over the next month, he was able to do this, and his physical condition improved still more.

The third time Jim came for prayer, he realized that he felt guilty for neglecting his mother during her last months. The healing team declared God's love and forgiveness, praying that Jim be able to feel this forgiving grace in his body, especially in his abdomen. The following time the team saw Jim, his pain was nearly gone, and he asked for prayers of thanksgiving for his healing.

Could the team have simply prayed for the healing of Jim's physical pain? Yes, of course, and perhaps his ulcer would have been healed. But because discernment plays an important part in identifying the root cause of illness, it led to Jim's being deeply healed in emotions and spirit, as well as body.

## When You Meet to Pray for Healing

We have been focusing on how to prepare spiritually for healing prayer and how to listen to God in a discernment process, letting our discernment shape our prayer. Now we turn our attention to the actual process of praying with another. Although prayers for healing can take place without the sufferer present, is it usually desirable to pray face-to-face for one in need. Doing so has several advantages. First, careful listening to the sufferer can help with discernment. Second, when you are physically present you can touch in a variety of ways. You can lay on hands or anoint with oil. You can give a hug or hold one who is crying. God uses our hands and bodies for healing, and touching often helps the one being prayed for to experience God's love. (We will say more below about laying on of hands and anointing.)

Finally, when you are actually with someone, you can listen and respond to the story of their suffering. You can declare forgiveness of sin. You can share your own faith. You can suggest soaking prayer or faith imagination. In other words, you can enter into a face-to-face pastoral relationship with the one for whom you are praying. (By "pastoral relationship" we refer to not only professional ministers but to all who share the grace of God with another.)

It is ideal to be able to spend enough time with people individually to hear them out before praying with them. When that is not possible, as during a healing service in which many people await prayer, we must depend even more fully on the Holy Spirit to supply what we lack.

When you have the opportunity for this intimate caring presence, it is crucial to be as sensitive and respectful as possible. The following guidelines are for those who find themselves in such a pastoring role.

1. Listen to the person who has sought healing. Let him or her know you are listening by putting the person's feelings in your own words. This can be part of the prayer itself or a brief comment you make before you pray. For example, a person may have had a cancer biopsy but does not yet have the results. Your response might be, "You sound so worried and scared." This sounds easy, but it takes lots of practice to do well. Friends can practice verbalizing feelings by listening to stories of each other's lives.[4]

2. Listen to God. Pay attention to whatever discernment may come to you even as the person speaks.

3. Do not give advice. You just might be wrong. Even if you are right, you risk making the person dependent on you.

4. Do not say, "I know just how you feel," even if you have been through a similar experience. Remember that each person's response is unique, and the person you are talking to may have reacted quite differently from you. Even if the difference is subtle, it must be respected.

5. Witness to your own faith as you feel led, but from an "I" position. Saying, "Don't you know that God loves you?" may make a sick person feel guilty and wrong. And saying, "Remember that God loves you," can sound preachy. But if you say, "I believe that God loves you," you are simply bearing witness to your own faith.

6. Allow the person to cry. Let yourself relax in the presence of tears. Often gentle tears are the lubrication of God's action in a person. Provide tissues, and let the Lord work.

7. As you pray with another, be comfortable with periods of silence. You do not have to think up beautiful words. The words you do say can be very simple. Trust that the Holy Spirit prays through you "with sighs too deep for words" (Rom. 8:26) and will give you whatever words you need.

8. When it seems helpful to pray for a person using soaking prayer, we run out of words very quickly. Then we can just sit in God's presence with our hands on the person, trusting God to be at work. During soaking prayer you can visualize or otherwise imagine the person with Jesus. Watch what Jesus does; listen to what he says. Pay attention to what emotion he seems to show. You might want to ask the person for whom you are praying to invite Jesus into his or her imagination.

9. Before you finish the prayer time, thank God for hearing you and for being at work in the person. In faith, ask God to continue the healing process.

## Healing Rituals

When used in connection with healing prayer, symbolic actions can be channels of God's grace, sending powerful messages to a person's inner being. The healing power of Jesus is released in special measure when prayers for healing are offered during the celebration of Holy Communion.

In addition to Holy Communion, other simple rituals are important vehicles for healing prayer. If those praying for another become comfortable with these rituals, the effectiveness of their ministry can be greatly enhanced.

The most common ritual in healing prayer is the *laying on of hands*. Touching is universally accepted as a way of saying, "I care about you. I love you." As when parents instinctively kiss or touch the place where a child hurts, God uses this natural response of touching to heal and to bless others. Jesus modeled this ancient practice for us. He often healed by putting his hands on a person, and the early church followed his example.

The model for the laying on of hands is the loving and respect-ful touch of a caring friend. Clearly it should be neither aggressive nor sexual, and it is done only with the explicit permission of the one receiving prayer. You may want to put your hands where the problem is located, if appropriate. Therefore, if the person has heart trouble, you may, with permission, want to touch his or her chest.

Some people may be self-conscious about touching or being touched. To help overcome this shyness try the laying on of hands a few times with a good friend. Many people find that it is natural and beautiful once they have had some experience with it. However, if you really cannot feel comfortable with laying on hands, or if someone does not want hands laid on them, by all means respect the feelings. Just pray, and trust God to work.

A second healing ritual is *confession and forgiveness*. When someone confesses sin in our presence, it is our privilege to declare God's forgiveness. We believe that any Christian can do this, for it is sim-ply a matter of attesting to God's willingness to forgive. You might say, "Whenever we confess our sins and are sorry, God always for-gives. In the name of Jesus Christ you are forgiven."

Forgiveness of sin is a beautiful way God works to heal our spir-itual brokenness. Quite often, being freed of crippling guilt paves the way for physical and emotional healing as well.

A third ritual of healing is anointing with oil. In the ancient world, oil was used for cosmetic and medicinal purposes (recall the Good Samaritan, Luke 10:34). In Israel, oil was used religiously in con-nection with the consecration of priests (Exod. 28:41), kings (1 Sam. 16:13), and those especially favored by God (Ps. 23:5). Anointing has been practiced in the Christian church since the beginning, and it symbolizes the giving of special divine blessing upon the one anointed. No wonder that anointing can be a deeply moving experience, like being filled with the balm of God's love.

When a person wishes to be anointed, simply dip your thumb or finger into the oil and rub it on the person's skin, perhaps making the sign of the cross with the oil. You may put the oil either where the problem is (for example, on a broken leg) or on the person's forehead or hand. You might say, "[Name], I anoint you for healing in the name of Jesus. Let this oil soaking into your skin remind you of God's love soaking into your whole being—body, emotions, and spirit."

## After the Amen

When you have finished a session of praying for another, it is important to let go. The following are suggestions for doing so.

1. As the prayer session ends, release the person prayed for to God's care. Give up any burden you have taken on and any need to have the person be made well according to your agenda. Ask God to heal any brokenness in you that has surfaced during the prayer. Then let God take care of you for a bit. Spend some time resting in God's presence, letting yourself be nourished.

2. Continue to pray for the person regularly, but guard against carrying the person as a burden. Let Jesus do the carrying. Your part is simply to love and pray.

3. Be absolutely trustworthy about keeping confidences. This means no one outside the prayer group should know anything that was said or done during the time of healing prayer. Nothing can destroy a healing ministry faster than to be careless in this respect.

4. Be sure to lighten up. As a healing ministry grows, it becomes increasingly vital to take regular time off for rest—for fun and silliness, for your own growth and creativity, for whatever renews you.

## *Julia: A Simple Story of Healing Prayer*

Perhaps all these suggestions and instructions seem a bit over-whelming. Actually, the practice of praying for another's healing feels very ordinary and simple. Much healing prayer takes place in informal ways in the normal context of friendship or family life. Often the prayers do not have to do with a crisis or with a grave illness, but just with the circumstances of day-to-day living. Healing prayer can flow naturally out of a minor event between two friends, as in this story of Tilda's.

One day my friend Julia and I planned to have lunch, then go to a large, empty parking lot near the beach. Julia had just received her learner's permit, which gave her the right to practice driving. We would have her first driving lesson in the parking lot with my car.

When I got to Julia's house, she answered the door limping, her face twisted in pain. Her knee had begun to hurt and swell just that morning. She could not imagine what was going on, as she had never before been troubled by her knee. Julia thought we might have to postpone the driving lesson because it was her right knee that was affected and she did not think she could use it for the accelerator and brake.

We decided to see whether praying for a few minutes might help. As we prayed for discernment, I began to see Julia's face in my mind's eye. Her eyes looked scared. Then I "saw" her hunched in the driver's seat, holding the steering wheel with white-knuckled tension.

I asked Julia if she was scared. She replied that as we were praying she realized that she was absolutely terrified of driving. She was afraid she would make some terrible mistake and that the car would "go crazy." She was afraid I would criticize and yell at her, as another teacher had. She knew these fears were not realistic, but they were there just the same. And it seemed that her fear was being expressed through pain in her knee. Both of us were well aware that the painful knee offered the perfect alibi for not having to drive that day. It "hurt too much."

We discerned that we needed to pray, not about the pain in her knee, but about her fear. I laid my hands on Julia's knee, and we prayed together that God would somehow address her fear of learning to drive. I said something like this, "God, you know how afraid Julia is right now, and you know how much her knee hurts. Please come into her fear and speak your truth into her heart. Heal her, Lord, of whatever is making her so afraid. Thank you for hearing us. . . ."

Then we sat in silence, waiting. After a few minutes, Julia said that she was seeing a picture of herself in the driver's seat, with Jesus sitting next to her, smiling, and obviously enjoying the ride. It seemed that he was telling her, without words, that he wanted her to have the freedom of a driver's license.

As Julia told me how Jesus seemed to be responding to our prayers, she began to breathe sighs of relief, and her body relaxed. Her face lost its tension. She began to smile. A few minutes later the pain in her knee was almost gone. By the time we finished lunch, she had no pain at all.

When we arrived at the parking lot for her lesson, Julia was still a little afraid. We needed to pause a few times to remember the powerful picture of Jesus sitting next to her and to thank him for his help. During subsequent lessons, her fear lessened. Today she has her own car and is a confident, safe driver.

## CHAPTER FIVE

# Social Healing: Praying for Institutions

Some years ago in Johannesburg, during the height of the apartheid regime in South Africa, Bob listened to a white South African pastor talk about his ministry. He worked mostly with blacks outside as well as within the church. Bob had seen firsthand how the pastor's daily life was an exhausting frenzy of activity, as he tried to meet endless needs for housing, jobs, and health care, as well as relief from government oppression and from every imaginable human need. Added to this, the pastor's life was in danger. His house had been raided by police, his office was later bombed. In his own white family he was something of an outcast. But, to his mind, his Christian activism was not extraordinary, but simply his response to the gospel in his situation.

The conversation turned to the pastor's inner religious life. Unconscious of the shift in tone, he described a simple, personal trust in God, a profound sense of being loved and led by Christ. God was real to him. When he spoke of the heavy pastoral counseling load he carried, it was in terms by now familiar to the readers of this book: he prayed for healing as if his prayers would make a difference.

Asked if he experienced a tension between his activism and his personal piety, the pastor strongly rejected such a distinction. Public ministry and private faith are absolutely inseparable, he insisted, and he could not conceive either apart from the other.

To those who struggle to hold together inner and outward expressions of faith, a testimony like that of this South African pastor is especially moving because it is lived at such a personal cost. He inspires us because his relationship to God is the very source of his intense social ministry.

So far in our exploration of healing prayer we have focused our attention on individuals. Why not? one might ask. Is it not the individual who is the focus of healing in the Bible and in traditional healing ministries? And do the problems of social organizations such as families, churches, corporations, and nations lend themselves to the kinds of activities we have been exploring thus far? How can we lay hands on social ills or anoint institutions?

While this focus upon individual healing may be more or less understandable, it is unfortunate. It keeps us from seeing the many ways God is involved in social healing. And so we may fail to call upon vital spiritual resources available in the struggle for justice and peace.

An exclusive focus upon individual healing is doubly unfortunate because it tends to perpetuate the split between the private and the public expressions of religious faith, between activists and pietists, what Elizabeth O'Connor called the inward and outward journeys.[1] We know in our hearts that dwelling upon only one of these is one-sided, a settling for merely part of the gospel. But we also know how easy it is to settle for a one-sided faith, given our differing religious visions, temperaments, and preferences.

The message of this chapter, however, is not just that activism and personal spirituality need to be held together. True as that is, our purpose here is more limited and more novel. We want to *explore the spiritual resources of Christian faith for healing the brokenness of social institutions.* Our question is this: Granted that Christian social activism is vitally important, is there something more than activism that the church can offer for the healing of social brokenness, something distinctive, something arising out of its unique vocation as the body of Christ? And if there is, how can the church go about imagining and instituting social healing of this kind?

This is a little-explored area where there are no experts. There are, however, provocative experiments and explorations that suggest much can be gained from raising these questions in the church.

## Healing: The Social Dimension

We begin with the obvious. Social institutions are in profound need of healing. Everywhere we look we see social brokenness and a deep need for God's grace to redeem not just individuals but the social structures in which individuals live their lives.

For example:

A family system is so dysfunctional that it makes no sense to ask who is at fault; the system itself is sick and all its members are in some sense both victims and perpetrators.

A congregation experiences internal conflict that seems to have a life of its own and lasts over many years as particular persons come and go.

A sovereign nation behaves toward some of its citizens in ways that rob them of basic human rights, even of their lives. It is not that some individuals or classes are inherently evil, rather that both oppressors and oppressed are trapped in systems of exploitation and suffering that diminish the humanity of all.

One has only to think of the social manifestations of the so-called seven deadly sins of pride, greed, lust, envy, gluttony, anger, and despair (traditionally called sloth). The effects of social brokenness are tragically evident everywhere: in the pollution of air, earth, and water; in the poverty, homelessness, and despair of inner cities; in the cheapened picture of life portrayed in mass media; in the chauvinism of nation, race, and group; in the addiction to weaponry and war. It is not an exaggeration to say that the places where we live, work, worship, volunteer, consume, and vote are enmeshed in sick social systems.

Most Christians believe the church should be directly involved in addressing social brokenness. We willingly vote, lobby, organize, advocate, and act for the transformation of society. The question is, is spiritual intervention also relevant? Are social systems appropriate objects of healing prayer?

We believe the answer is a resounding yes. Recall the definition of healing in chapter 1: "healing is a process that involves the totality of our being—body, mind, emotion, spirit, and our social context." While this could be taken to refer only to the healing of the individual *in* society, we here emphasize a more inclusive sense. Healing is a process that involves our social contexts, the healing *of* society.

The social dimension of healing is well stated in a paper of the Christian Medical Commission of the World Council of Churches. "Health and wholeness, it says," is "a dynamic state of well-being of the individual and the society; of physical, mental, spiritual, economic, political, and social well-being; of being in harmony with each other, with the natural environment and with God."[2]

## Biblical Perspectives on Social Healing

*Hebrew Bible.* The biblical God cares about and intervenes on behalf of the community. This is evident in the very concept of *shalom,* peace. In the Hebrew Bible Yahweh is portrayed as desiring the *shalom* of Israel as a whole. *Shalom* in the biblical perspective is vastly different from inner tranquility or peace and quiet. Rather, *shalom* describes a dynamic condition of social wholeness marked by justice, loyalty, and solidarity.[3] The Bible records myriad stories that illumine God's desire to heal both individuals and social institutions.

After leading Israel out of Egypt, Yahweh caused bitter water to be purified and said to the people, "I am the LORD who heals you" (Exod. 15:26). Yahweh's healing consisted both of preserving the people's physical health and liberating them from Pharaoh's bondage.[4] This is healing indeed. On other occasions in the wilderness period, Yahweh acted on behalf of the people as a whole, providing quails and manna to eat (Exod. 16), water to drink (Exod. 17), and various means of purification and atonement for the sins of the people (Lev. 16; Num. 19).

The prophets speak of the redeeming work of Yahweh as a kind of healing. Malachi promises: "For you who revere my name the sun of righteousness shall rise, with healing in its wings" (Mal. 4:2). Second Isaiah speaks of the Servant of the Lord, upon whom was laid "the punishment that *made us whole,* and by his bruises *we are healed*" (Isa. 53:5, emphasis added).

*New Testament.* In the Gospels, Jesus' healing of individual sufferers is a familiar theme. The healing of social institutions is not so explicit. Yet a closer look reveals a richer picture. The central message of Jesus' preaching is the announcement of the coming *basileia* of God. Sometimes translated "kingdom," *basileia* is both the realm where God holds sway (a domain or sphere of influence) and God's *rule* over humanity (a relationship of sovereign authority). As such, the *basileia* of God is a thoroughly social and corporate reality. The central thrust of Jesus' proclamation of the *basileia* of God was *the restoration of Israel as a people* in the realm where God is sovereign.

Jesus' healings of individual persons were, taken together, manifestations of God's *basileia*. As New Testament scholar John Meier writes, Jesus' deeds of power "both proclaimed and actualized, however imperfectly, the kingdom of God promised by the prophets."[5] Inevitably, Jesus' healings of individuals would have had social consequences. When Jesus stretched out his hand to heal a leper by means of touch (Mark 1:40-42), his gesture crossed an abyss of fear and religious taboo. It sent the message that such a one was not to be outcast, as was the custom, but was included in a new community marked by compassion for all. When he called an impure woman "daughter," he gave her a new status and identity in a newly formed family of equals (Mark 5:25-34). When Jesus drove the demons named Legion from the man who dwelt among the tombs (and the two thousand swine into the sea!), his act served notice that no military occupation (Legion!) should presume to rival God's sovereign rule of the people of Palestine. Reading between the lines we see Jesus casting out political and economic demons along with the personal demons of the affected man (Mark 5:1-20).[6]

The event of Jesus "casting out" the money changers from the Temple is a kind of social exorcism (Mark 11:15-17).[7] Through this prophetic action Jesus "cleansed" the Temple by exposing to the light of divine revelation the sin of the Temple leadership. Social healing in this instance was a public truth-telling of God's sovereign judgment upon a sacred institution gone astray.

Paul and his followers were keenly aware of the social dimensions of the conflict with evil. The church's struggle, they warned, is "against the rulers, against the authorities, against the cosmic powers of this present darkness, against the spiritual forces of evil in the heavenly places" (Eph. 6:12; see Eph. 6:10-17; Gal. 4:3, 8f.; Col. 1:15f.). Against these the church must arm itself spiritually as against worldly armies.

In the Book of Revelation, the Roman Empire, symbolized as the whore Babylon, is the earthly embodiment of evil. The entire Book of Revelation can be read as an exorcism of the great dragon Satan and his minion, Babylon. In the end Christ triumphs over Babylon's oppression and idolatry. One can scarcely imagine a more scathing spiritual indictment of evil committed by the state, or a more powerful claiming of victory over it. Through the media of imaginative poetry, prophetic vision, and song, the truth about Roman rule is told in such a way as to comfort and encourage early Christians, then an oppressed minority. Social evil, embodied in the state, was confronted, exposed, and dispatched in what could be called a creative act of social healing.

These few examples from the scriptures of Israel and the church are relevant to social healing today. They show, sometimes between the lines but often explicitly, that (1) *God wills the healing and transformation not only of individuals but also of the social institutions in which individuals exist;* and (2) *the people of God have available a variety of means of spiritual intervention to accomplish social healing in God's name.*

## Imagining Social Healing—Two Stories

It is one thing to recognize that our understanding of healing should extend to the social realm and that God indeed wills the healing of churches and nations. It is something else to imagine how we can intervene spiritually for social healing. What does it mean to *pray* for social healing? How does such prayer differ from social action? How does it differ from ordinary intercessory prayer?

Two actual cases may help us begin to imagine concrete acts of praying for institutional healing.

## The Drowned Church

*Description.* A pastor was frustrated and baffled by the pervasive mood of hopelessness and negativity that had gripped her congregation for years. Nothing she tried seemed to help. "It won't work here," was the church's constant refrain. Also, the bitterness and strife among some members was all too evident as they lingered in the narthex before the worship service, openly arguing and trading insults. The pastor tried to counter the prevailing mood with good programming; Bible studies, prayer groups, and other activities that might build up the church, quickly died from lack of interest. The pastor came to believe that the church as a whole was somehow sick, that there was an indefinable malaise blocking its growth and health.

Seeking support, the pastor asked a small group of clergy friends, people not associated with the congregation, to gather with her late one afternoon when no parishioners would be in the church. The plan was to pray for the healing of the church and discern the underlying sources of the church's malaise. They would also celebrate Holy Communion for the healing of the congregation.

As the pastor's friends gathered, one was drawn to a commemorative plaque in a hallway. It stated that the church building had been erected at the expense of the local state government. Questions about this unusual funding source prompted the pastor to tell a story of institutional trauma. The original church building had been condemned by the state in order to build a dam and form a lake in the area. The state had paid for the relocation of the church building to its present site. At the time the church members had not liked the move but had no say in the state's action. Everything of value had been removed, and the shell of the church building was covered by the waters of the newly formed lake. All this had occurred almost a generation before. A few of the present members were children at the time of the move, but most had no direct memory of it. As the prayer group heard the story, one of them called it the story of the "drowned church."

The prayer group began by opening itself to the guidance of the Holy Spirit in order to discern how to shape their prayers and acts of intercession. What was the spiritual malaise the congregation suffered? As the group meditated about the church's experience, it was the image of the drowned church that came forward. It seemed the institution had suffered a trauma, just as an individual might. The church had a buried collective memory of losing something dear and holy. The grieving and sense of loss and helplessness lived on in the institution, expressed in the undertone of defeat, negativism, and bitterness.

The prayer group was led to pray for the healing of the congregation's memory, specifically that the waters that had meant drowning and death to the church would be transformed into baptismal waters leading to new life. Later, as a symbolic expression of this institutional baptismal renewal, members of the prayer group moved through the church from room to room, sprinkling water in a gesture of blessing. Even as they did this, the oppressive atmosphere they had earlier sensed in the building seemed to lighten.

During Holy Communion, the group prayed for the healing of the congregation as a whole and for specific individuals who seemed to be lightening rods for contention. They prayed for the pastor, that she herself be freed from any attitudes or behavior that perpetuated the church's illness. At the end, as a sign and anticipation of the church's renewal, the group rang the church bell, loudly and joyfully.

The pastor later reported what happened after the group's spiritual intervention. The very next Sunday no one stood arguing and gossiping in the narthex before the service. Instead, the people were in the pews, many of them praying! In the days immediately following the service, the pastor was astonished and delighted when several people, independent of each other, told her that they would like to see the church start a Bible study. Although such a spurt of interest did not last, it marked the point at which things began to turn around.

Within a year, many new people had come into the church, and the lay leadership had almost completely changed. There was a new openness and generosity among the people. The church trustees had reversed themselves on forbidding Alcoholics Anonymous and other self-help groups from using the church facilities.

One of the most significant changes was what the pastor called "a turn in the pastor's heart," so that she felt both more rooted and more protected. The pastor believes a connection existed between these striking changes in behavior and attitude and the prayers and symbolic acts of the healing service.

Three years later, while the church was still in need of continued healing, in many ways it was a different church than it had been. A solid core of active laypeople was committed to the church, and a weekly healing service continued prayers for its healing.

The prayers for the drowned church initiated a time of turning for the congregation. All the problems were not miraculously solved. But from that time on a shift of attitude, an opening to a new spirit and a new life, was made possible.

Reflection. What the pastor and her friends did was a form of prayer on behalf of the congregation. Of course, many people pray for institutions to which they belong. But this was different from what we usually think of as intercessory prayer.

To begin with, their intervention arose out of the conviction that prayer for the institution as an institution could make a difference. The group was prepared to think of the church as a kind of corporate person, with a history and a memory and a capacity for being hurt. They were led to this conviction not by an appeal to a sociological theory but from their belief that God loved that congregation for itself and desired that it be whole.

Second, the pastor gathered a group to pray with her. These were not consultants and problem solvers, important as such people are, but people of prayer, discerners whose task was to be open to the inner spiritual dynamics of the congregation. As many people can attest, spiritual effectiveness is higher in a group gathered for prayer than in an individual praying alone. More than that, usually a greater capacity for spiritual discernment exists within a group than in an individual.

Third, discernment formed an essential part of the group's praying. In social healing, discernment is a crucial beginning step toward opening ourselves intentionally to the way the Holy Spirit wants to work in the situation.

Fourth, once the group's discernment had suggested a direction for their prayer, *ritual* played a key role in their work. In celebrating Holy Communion on behalf of the church, in sprinkling the church rooms with water in an action reminiscent of baptism, even in pealing the church bell, the group expressed their intercession through intentional words and deeds. They acted in the prayerful hope that God would use their actions for the good of the church. Many people involved in praying for healing find, time and again, how rituals—the historic rites and ceremonies of the church as well as acts designed specially for specific needs—are powerful means whereby God effects healing.

Fifth, the group *prayed for particular persons*, including the pastor. Institutional healing does not overlook the needs or the responsibilities of individuals who comprise the group, nor does it look for scapegoats. Just as we hold together body, mind, and spirit, so we hold together institutional structures and the people within them.

Two further reflections are in order. The pastor's asking for these prayers was not an alternative to other means of addressing the church's problems. Enriched preaching and Christian education, conflict management, and other community healing interventions were important for that congregation. What this case does illustrate is the validity of a both/and approach to social healing, just as in personal healing. It is important to include intentional and imaginative acts of prayer among the many ways we seek to bring wholeness to institutions in which we live and work.

Finally, it surely will be in the minds of some readers that we cannot rationally explain what happened in the case of the drowned church. We cannot objectively demonstrate a clear-cut cause-and-effect relationship between the prayer group's intervention and subsequent changes. An elusive, inexplicable quality marks the events. For some this may be grounds for dismissing the whole episode as wishful thinking or coincidence. Increasing numbers of Christians, however, are not put off by their inability to explain the grace that seems to embrace us. After all, God's ways of working in human affairs are always elusive and mysterious! Rather, we sense the promise in such events and take the risk of praying in faith without needing to understand how God uses our prayers. Those who prayed for the drowned church entered into a ritual of social healing, sensing that this somehow released the healing power of God in the situation. That was enough for them to go on.

## Social Exorcism

The Reverend Dr. George D. McClain is a social activist in the United Methodist Church, and he served for many years as the executive secretary of the Methodist Federation for Social Action. A few years ago he was led to employ a form of spiritual intervention against social evil that was at once innovative (as a means of social transformation) and traditional (in its biblical roots). We here draw upon an account he has written of these activities.[8]

*Description.* George D. McClain developed what he calls "social exorcism" in the course of organizing a public demonstration against apartheid in front of the South African consulate in New York City in March 1 985. In addition to the usual prayers, speeches, and hymns, George led the assembled group in a declaration renouncing the spiritual power wielded by apartheid:

> We act today, in the name of Jesus Christ, to break the power of sin and death.

We declare that in Jesus Christ the power of apartheid is broken and in the fullness of time will fall.

We therefore renounce any power that apartheid in South Africa may have over our personal lives, over the United Methodist Church, its agencies and conferences, over our investments or programs, or over our local churches and our ministries within them.[9]

Uttered in the context of Christian ritual, the statement recognized that apartheid is an ideology with its own spiritual power. The statement dealt with this spiritual power in a manner appropriate to Christian faith, declaring it ultimately subject to Christ and renouncing any personal or institutional complicity with it.

To people accustomed to dealing with social and political issues as "problems" to be solved through the usual avenues of "social action," such a ritual declaration may seem quaintly irrelevant. George McClain certainly felt the strangeness of it. Trained in the theological traditions of Paul Tillich and Karl Barth, he was led only slowly to social exorcism by a growing conviction that church people tend to have a limited vision of the church's unique role in social transformation.

All too seldom have we prayed for institutional transformation, . . . with an expectation that our prayers would be answered. And all too seldom have we paused quietly to discern either the root cause of the problem—the problem behind the problem—or what God wanted us—uniquely us—to do about it in that moment.[10]

A further impetus to McClain's work was a growing conviction about the nature of evil, that evil is not just the absence of good but, within individuals, can manifest an "independent, aggressive, God-defying quality." Further, he reasoned, if evil has this quality, then it seemed that the power of Christ to cast out the emissaries of this evil was not just a sort of embarrassing and undigested aspect of the New Testament's witness, but a real necessity.

And in terms of my own social action ministry I began to ask the question, "Are not institutions, as well as persons, often held captive by evil powers; and if so, what is the ministry of the church toward them?"[11]

McClain's experiments with this approach to confronting social evil continued in a confrontation with a particular denominational agency charged with investing church pension funds. Against the wishes of the governing body of the denomination, and most vocal opinion in the church, the agency was refusing to divest its stock holdings in companies doing business in South Africa or even to press companies to stop doing business with the apartheid economy. Despite numerous attempts by anti-apartheid activists to influence the agency, including resolutions, petitions, meetings, picketing, and civil disobedience, the situation was at an impasse.

In a summer retreat setting during this time, McClain and a few associates expressed their deep frustration and sense of failure. Some members of the group were experienced with liturgies of deliverance for individuals, and one of them suggested that the group, then and there, hold a ritual of social exorcism modeled on a service of individual exorcism. In this way they would seek God's help in breaking the chains that linked the church and its agency with apartheid.

The social exorcism service began with discerning the identity of the ungodly spirits blocking the church. The group concluded that they were the spirits of fear and intimidation, arrogance and lust for power, mammon, and patriarchy. A statement of purpose included these words:

We gather . . . to proclaim Jesus Christ as the ultimate authority over all beings, structures, and institutions. All spirits, influences, or powers, recognized or unrecognized, which are not of God, are in principle defeated or self-defeating and have in Christ been exposed as fraudulent. We offer ourselves as instruments of God's power and sovereignty over the power of evil.[12]

There followed the reading of Colossians 1:16, which declares the authority of Christ over all the powers of the created order. The group then confessed any ways in which they were in complicity with the spirits they had identified. Following the sharing of Bread and Cup, they spoke solemn words severing any ties between the agency and past negative influences, as well as solemn words casting out the spirits whose negative influence had been discerned, for example:

Spirit of fear and intimidation, in the name of Jesus Christ, we order you to depart from [the agency] and go to Jesus.[13]

The service continued with prayers of support and renewal for the individual members of the agency. Finally, the group concluded with prayers for each other in their roles in the anti-apartheid struggle.

Exhausted after the lengthy service, McClain and the others sensed the power of the ritual in which they participated, and they felt that something within themselves had changed.

The following weeks brought an unexpected, dramatic change in the situation. The key figure in the agency's long-held divestment policy quite unexpectedly announced plans to resign. Suddenly there was an opportunity for a new policy under new leadership. Could that little group of activists claim a relationship between their service of social exorcism and that resignation and subsequent events? George McClain writes, "This connection may not be deduced through ordinary cause-effect analysis, but in terms of the 'logic' of the Spirit and her movement among us, I believe there was a powerful relationship."[14]

That was not the last of the surprises. At a meeting three months later, decision makers in the agency itself showed a perceptible change in their attitude toward the issue of divestment and toward the activists. That changed attitude continued through the following months, expressed in positive steps to bring the agency's policy in line with the wishes of the denomination as a whole. On their part, McClain and the other activists experienced a kind of conversion in their attitudes toward the members of the agency, seeing them not as adversaries but as men and women trying to carry out a difficult trust to the best of their abilities. McClain and others continued to act in the belief that the struggle was not simply a matter of policy advocacy but of an engagement with spiritual powers.

It is important to note that the activists were not identifying particular members as evil persons. McClain wrote of the members of the agency:

Actually we believe them to be dedicated, responsible, even exem- plary, Christian people. Rather we address this board collectively as trustees of an institution which is blocked from doing God's will in relation to South African investments. In this regard the board is held captive by alien influences and stands in need of a healing ministry which we here seek to perform.[15]

George McClain's own reflections on social exorcism provide a fitting conclusion to this story. "This whole experience suggests to me very strongly that we need to employ our spiritual gifts as part of our witness to God's transforming love and power." He concludes:

> Walter Brueggemann suggests that in our era God is at work dismantling the Enlightenment worldview, with its unduly rationalistic, controlling, and dominating characteristics. I find his assertion quite illuminating, for it witnesses to a living God who is inviting us to a more complete view of the universe as physical and spiritual. The shattering of our overly rationalistic worldview is part of that invitation. Only then can we begin to place the full range of our spiritual life and gifts at God's disposal in the struggle for the social transformation which God is stirring up.[16]

*Reflection.* This case has several things in common with the drowned church: (1) A group acted in the belief that their prayers could make a difference. (2) It was crucial that the group gathered as the body of Christ. They benefited from shared insights and provided a check against individual distortion. (3) Their first act was to try to discern the true spiritual situation, the problem behind the problem. (4) In response, they drew upon and modified traditional rituals of the church (in this case, Holy Communion and exorcism). (5) They acted on behalf of individuals as well as the institution as a whole and did not overlook their own need for forgiveness and healing.

The case has unique aspects, as well, arising especially out of the participants' willingness to think about social evil in a certain way. They acted in the belief that evil has an aggressive, God-defying character. When they saw apartheid not only as a set of political and economic arrangements but also as a veritable legion of evil spirits arrayed against God and working ill against all who are touched by them, then the possibility was opened for a deeper and more telling assault than that offered by political measures alone.[17] Seeing evil in this way, the group acted on the basis of the New Testament faith in Christ's victory over Satan. In essence, their services of social exorcism were declarations of the way things are under God.

Social exorcism is truly an act of faith in the ultimate triumph of righteousness. Its authority resides in its connection to divine truth, which, when told, may begin to transform the present moment.

The spiritual power of social exorcism resides in the victory of Christ over sin and death. Christians confess that no structure of society, no "principality or power," lies outside the sphere of God's creative and redemptive care. Hard as this may be to believe in regard to individual brokenness, it is even harder to affirm in the face of the massive human suffering brought on by social evil. How are we to reconcile this faith with the testimony of our senses, which, for example, saw apartheid flourishing for years after its demons had been exorcised in the name of Christ? What, after all, is transacted in a ritual of social exorcism?

First, and importantly, social exorcism is an *act of revelation*, in which evil is unmasked and the truth is told. We can scarcely overestimate the importance of prophetic truth telling, speaking the truth to power. Walter Wink writes in *Unmasking the Powers*:

> The march across the Selma bridge by black civil rights advocates was an act of exorcism. It exposed the demon of racism, stripping away the screen of legality and custom for the entire world to see. . . . the act is efficacious simply by virtue of its bearing witness to the truth in a climate of lies. . . . But the point of collective exorcism is not in the first place reform, but revelation: the unveiling of unsuspected evil in high places.[18]

Second, and equally important, social exorcism is *an act whereby evil is addressed and dealt with on a spiritual level.* The spiritual intervention makes a difference, for the realm of evil has been defeated by Christ. The attitude of a church agency changed subtly but significantly, and new possibilities were opened. This is not to be understood in rational cause-effect ways but in what George McClain calls "the logic of the Spirit." God used the prayers and rituals of the community to work creatively for healing. As with virtually all our experience of the grace of God, we participate in it and receive its benefits before we understand what we have experienced.

## Holding a Service of Social Exorcism

We offer the following service as a model of a group process of social exorcism within the setting of a service of worship.

Social exorcism is to be entered into soberly, prayerfully, and expectantly. It is not a way to make an institution do what you want, but a way of cooperating with God's will for the institution.

Because so much depends on group discernment in social exorcism, the congregation literally "works through" the various components of the service. There will be times of silent and verbal reflection as well as liturgical movement. Much of the process will arise from the congregation, with the leaders suggesting the general flow.

The service below is meant for a group of about twelve persons or less. To adapt it for a larger group, let a small group do most of the discernment ahead of time, but remain open for new discernment as the service proceeds.

We strongly recommend that Holy Communion be included in the service. Our experience is that God's grace seems to be poured out in greater measure when we pray in the context of Communion. Communion also focuses the congregation's attention on the power of Christ rather than on a fascination with demonic powers.

Those who will participate in the service should decide ahead of time on the institution that will be the focus of prayer. Any institution may be named—a family or church, school or business, a multinational corporation, an agency or branch of government, an ideology or social pattern that has institutional expression. Information about the institution's history and present life should be gathered if it is not already known to the group.

## A Service of Social Exorcism[19]

**Hymn**
**Invocation and Introduction**
After the opening prayer, briefly tell about the process of social exorcism, and outline what will happen in the service. Take a few minutes to answer or discuss any questions.

**Scripture**
Options: Exodus 15:13-20; Colossians 1:15-20; Mark 11:15-17.

**Discernment**
Begin with prayer that God will speak to you as a group, giving you what you need to know in order to pray with boldness for the healing and cleansing of the institution. Briefly share the history of the institution, especially any painful or traumatic events. Share

why this institution needs healing now.

1. Enter into a time of silence to discern the powers' identity. Ask the Holy Spirit: What has hurt or traumatized this institution? What are the spiritual forces at work? What are they called? (Listen for names, such as Arrogance, Greed, Patriarchy, Despair, or Cynicism.) In silence, be open to any images, ideas, words, or feelings that come.

Share the discernment and list on newsprint the names of the spiritual forces at work.

2. Note any traumas or pain suffered by the institution.

3. Confront the powers within. Returning to silence, each person asks the Holy Spirit: What stands in the way of my being free of these powers? How am I myself in collusion with them? Examine motives, ambitions, addictions. For example, if what you have named is a spirit of greed, ponder how you allow greed into your own life.

**Confession and Absolution**
Take time to confess these things together, silently or aloud, and hear a declaration of God's forgiveness.

**Holy Communion**

**Words of Deliverance**
1. Invoke the protection of Christ from the aggressive assault of the powers. Ask that no person or object be harmed as a consequence of this service of exorcism.

2. Put on the whole armor of God by reading aloud Ephesians 6:10-20, asking each person to see himself or herself being armed by God.

3. Read together:

We discern that there are influences and spirits not of God which are preying upon [institution] and holding it captive to alien principalities and powers.

In the name and power of Jesus Christ we bind these spirits and powers not of God so that they can do no more evil.

We name [read the names of the spirits] and declare they are bound by the power of Jesus Christ. We declare that they are exposed, discredited, and stripped of their power.

In the name and power of Jesus Christ we declare that all ties have now been severed between [institution] and any previous incidents, influences, history, policies, traditions, theories, customs, authorities, financial or political groups, government institutions or individuals who have become conduits, advisors, or channels, misdirecting this institution or using it or persons who are connected to it for ungodly ends.

Let us now order the ungodly spirits to depart. [Using the following words, order each spirit away individually, by name. You may sense that some spirits need to be addressed more than once.]

Spirit of [Name], in the name and power of Jesus Christ we order you to depart immediately and completely from [institution], and surrender before God.

[Repeat for each Spirit by name].

## Prayer of Healing and Thanksgiving

Pray for the healing of any traumas suffered by the institution, and that the institution be renewed in its God-given purpose. Pray for the people in the institution, both the forces for good and the disrupters, that they find their way to serve the purpose of the institution with humility and grace. Give thanks for what God will do, and release your efforts to be used by God.

## Hymn

## Benediction

## CHAPTER SIX

# The Church as a Healing Community

H ealthy churches are healing communities in three inter-connected senses.

Healing communities are *communities of people who know they need healing*. People broken in spirit, body, mind, or relationships gather to find support and healing.

Second, healing communities are *communities in process of being healed*. In them reconciliation, liberation, justice, and peace are emerging as qualities of community life.

Third, healing communities are *communities of healers*. People in such communities stretch out their hands to persons and institutions in obedience to Christ.

In this chapter we draw upon two remarkable biblical portraits to evoke a sense of what it might mean for churches to become healing communities. Then, we look practically at how to start a healing ministry in a local church.

## Summoning the Elders

In the Letter of James is a passage unfamiliar to many mainline

Protestants. It is one of the earliest descriptions of a church of wounded healers who are being healed themselves.

> Are any among you suffering? They should pray. Are any cheerful? They should sing songs of praise. Are any among you sick? They should call for the elders of the church and have them pray over them, anoint- ing them with oil in the name of the Lord. The prayer of faith will save the sick, and the Lord will raise them up; and anyone who has commit- ted sins will be forgiven. Therefore confess your sins to one another, and pray for one another, so that you may be healed. The prayer of the righteous is powerful and effective (James 5:13-16).

A Presbyterian minister tells about a parishioner in a church he served in western Pennsylvania many years ago. Tom was a faithful, longtime member of the church who was suffering from cranial cancer. He had lost his sight in one eye and full use of his limbs on one side of his body. Surgeons had done all they could. The prognosis was further diminishment ending in Tom's certain death.

One day Tom called the pastor to say that he had lost hope in medical care. He had read a passage in the Letter of James where he discovered that "the prayer of faith will save the sick, and the Lord will raise them up; and anyone who has committed sins will be for- given." And so, though it was a departure from the traditions of his church, he asked the pastor to convene elders, come to the hospital, and anoint him with oil and pray over him.

This was something new for the pastor. But sensing that it could be reassuring to Tom, he summoned the elders and bought oil at the drugstore.

The elders were also surprised by Tom's request. Never before had they been asked to play this pastoral role. Yet they readily agreed to come and pray, glad for a way of expressing their concern for their friend. Perhaps, too, they sensed that in this way God could use them to help Tom.

So the pastor and elders gathered around Tom's hospital bed. They read the passage from James, laid hands on Tom, and prayed over him. The pastor touched his forehead with oil in the name of Jesus. Tom made a confession of sin and heard the group pronounce God's forgiving love. When they were finished nothing dramatic happened—to no one's particular surprise—but Tom seemed to be at peace.

After the anointing service, Tom did not regain the use of his eye or limbs, but from that time the progress of the cancer was arrested. To the amazement of his doctors, his pastor, and the whole congregation, Tom survived, and more than two decades later he was alive to tell one and all about his wonderful service of anointing!

Tom's remarkable story highlights the importance of the local church as the locus of Christian healing. For his part, Tom acted on a kind of intuitive wisdom, boldly asking for what he needed from the church. And the church in the person of the pastor and elders somehow had the grace to let itself be used by God. Whatever mixture of compassion, obedience, and awkwardness the pastor and elders brought to the moment, God used it all for Tom's good. What happened to Tom reminds us that *the church is truly the church when it puts itself at God's disposal and lets the Holy Spirit use it to heal and transform.*

Let the story of Tom's healing and the passage from the Letter of James plant some seeds for thinking of the church as a healing community. First, Tom was a loyal churchman who somehow knew where he needed to be in his hour of need, namely, surrounded by the church—literally! He might have traveled to a large healing service led by someone with a "gift of healing." Many people, sensing that their local church may not be open to healing prayer, attend such services, and some are helped. The appeal of the James passage is that it directed Tom to the community where he had always sought God's grace and where, he decided, he would seek it again. *Every Christian congregation has the potential for being a community where healing takes place.*

It is striking that those ordinary Presbyterian elders had a role in Tom's extraordinary healing. We may assume that they exercised spiritual trusteeship in the congregation as elders are supposed to do, but surely in their own eyes they possessed no special powers, no healing gifts. They did not need to, and that is the point.

The Letter of James reflects its roots in ancient Judaism, which had great confidence in the power of a righteous person's prayer. But we should not suppose that only "righteous" elders are worthy to do what Tom's friends did, or that people need some great measure of faith to be used in healing. The elders' obedience, not their righteousness, is what is impressive. We might even say that obedience was their special form of righteousness. It was what we might call "ordinary obedience," the kind each of us can imagine living out in our religious communities, without pretense or heroics. *Christian churches are called to become communities of ordinary obedience to the Spirit's healing activity in their midst.*

Praying for Tom's healing was already a stretch for the elders, but there is another, subtler shade of obedience in the story of Tom's healing. Tom surprised his pastor by appealing to the little-known religious rite of anointing described in James 5. The elders too were probably a bit taken back by the idea. But in the end they gave themselves to the enactment of the rite, out of some sense of faithfulness to the plain sense of the scriptural word.

We who pride ourselves on being modern and "with it" may find the elders' actions almost embarrassingly naive. But those with experience in healing ministries can testify that the Spirit addresses us through the plain sense of the Bible when we open ourselves to it. This is especially so when we imaginatively and expectantly enter the Gospel healing stories. Of course, we affirm solid biblical study, which is essential for the interpretation of Scripture in the church. But when in simplicity as the church we give ourselves to the enactment of the biblical words, we often find that the Spirit uses us and works through us for healing.

Finally, notice the strong connection in James 5 between healing and forgiveness. We have already seen in chapter 3 that an inability to forgive or accept forgiveness can erect a barrier to physical and emotional healing, and that confession and forgiveness can lead to deep spiritual healing. In James 5 the emphasis rests on a community setting in which sin is confessed and forgiveness pronounced.

Modern Christian communities offer a variety of settings in which persons feel free to confess their sin and seek forgiveness and reconciliation. In many churches confession and forgiveness happen regularly in worship through spoken acts. In addition, pastoral counseling and spiritual direction can provide opportunities to confess sin and receive forgiveness in more intimate settings. In these settings, the whole church is represented in the pastoral and priestly office.

The author of the Letter of James was wise in the ways of the human soul and knew the difference between curing a disease and healing the whole person. In the latter, the sufferer's relation to God and neighbor is always an indispensable factor. Healing that is Christian always reaches into the moral and spiritual dimensions of life. *It is part of the unique vocation of the Christian community to minister to the whole person.*

## *A Partnership of Giving and Receiving*

Healing that is Christian also encompasses the practical affairs of life: matters of health, welfare, and daily sustenance. One of the most vivid New Testament portrayals of a healing church might not even be identified as such at first glance. Nothing is said in Scripture about great miracles of healing being performed among the Christians of ancient Philippi. But their generosity and faithful service to their beloved apostle Paul were nothing less than a ministry of holistic healing. He writes to them:

> You Philippians indeed know that in the early days of the gospel, when I left Macedonia, *no church shared with me in the matter of giving and receiving,* except you alone. For even when I was in Thessalonica, you sent me help for my needs more than once. . . . I have been paid in full and have more than enough; I am fully satisfied, now that I have received from Epaphroditus the gifts you sent, a fragrant offering, a sacrifice acceptable and pleasing to God (Phil. 4:15-16, 18, emphasis added).

What did the church do for Paul? More than once they sent gifts of money to support him in his missionary work. Paul was proud that he had accepted no help from the Corinthians (1 Cor. 9:3-15; 2 Cor. 11:7-9). But with the Philippians he entered into a partnership of giving and receiving.

This partnership also included moral support during some of Paul's most difficult days. Even as he wrote, he did not know whether he would survive his imprisonment: "for all of you share in God's grace with me, both in my imprisonment and in the defense and confirmation of the gospel" (Phil. 1:7).

The church expressed partnership most concretely by sending one of its members, Epaphroditus, to minister to Paul on their behalf. Paul calls Epaphroditus "your messenger and minister to my need," and "my brother and co-worker and fellow soldier" (2:25). He nearly died while with Paul, "risking his life to make up for those services that you could not give me" (2:30). Others from Philippi, including the women activists Euodia and Syntyche, also labored alongside Paul on behalf of the church (4:2-4).

Undergirding all the practical support Paul received from the Philippians were their constant prayers on his behalf. He will continue to rejoice, he says, "for I know that through your prayers and the help of the Spirit of Jesus Christ this [imprisonment] will turn out for my deliverance" (1:19).

The church in Philippi stretched out its hands to sustain and support its friend in the specific ways he most urgently needed. In doing so they too become recipients of grace. They had already received much from Paul: their very existence as believers. He promised more. "My God will fully satisfy every need of yours according to his riches in glory in Christ Jesus" (4:19). Truly, the Philippians experienced being a healing community in a partnership of giving and receiving.

*A modern partnership.* A struggling, inner-city United Methodist church entered into a partnership of giving and receiving with a woman named Maria. Her story at first seems utterly removed from Paul and the Philippians. Beneath the surface, however, weaves a common theme.

Because of hospital overcrowding, the intensive care unit of a state mental hospital released Maria onto the streets. She had known a lifetime of neglect and cruel abuse and at the time of her release was seriously impaired socially and emotionally. Soon she came to the attention of the United Methodist church in her neighborhood. By then she was a young single mother, living on welfare and completely unequipped to take care of herself and her infant child. Maria's one anchor was a skillful therapist willing to work with her without pay.

But Maria needed help in managing the daily affairs of her life to sustain her through years of therapy and adjustment. Some church members stretched out their hands to Maria and her child with countless deeds of practical love. They gave her rides to the doctor and to the welfare office, provided baby-sitting, rustled up clothing for the child. They helped find secondhand furniture for her apartment and patiently taught her the basics of money management. They prayed for her at the monthly healing service. Through it all they became companions, friends who lent a sympathetic ear. Maria was an emotionally needy person, too draining for one or two people to deal with for very long. But the church community could distribute Maria's needs among them and in that way hang in with her.

Six years after her release from the hospital, Maria was still on a healing journey. But all the church's time and love and companionship—plus her therapist's help—had made a big difference. She was taking courses at a local college and seeking a part-time job. Her child was well-adjusted and doing well in school. She was a confident adult with a rapidly growing sense of self-worth and a feeling of hope about the future.

That is not the end of the story, however. Naturally gregarious, Maria had befriended the woman minister of a nearby storefront church. When the little church lost its lease, Maria brought the minister to her own United Methodist friends with the suggestion that they lease space to the storefront church. The United Methodist congregation could use the little bit of added income and so an agreement was reached, to the delight of all parties. Maria proved to be an angel to both congregations! Later, she produced beautiful drawings for the church's anniversary celebration. Though no one could have predicted Maria's future when the church people first began to reach out to her, the church and she entered into a partnership of giving and receiving.

*Whether in acts of prayer or deeds of service, a healing church is one that asks how the Spirit wants to work in the lives it touches and then makes itself available for that work.* A healing church sees that doing God's work in human lives always leads to healing, whether the healing of bodies and minds, giving money, supporting one in need with practical deeds of love, or giving people time and space to grow. Not least, a healing church knows itself to be the recipient of gifts from a God who, as Paul says, will supply its every need out of the riches of Jesus Christ.

## How to Start a Healing Ministry in Your Local Church

At this point let us shift gears from sparking imaginations to realistic planning.

Suppose you are beginning to envision your local church as a healing community. Though the idea may scare you a bit, you see it as a natural and exciting response to Jesus' invitation to stretch out your hand. You sense the spiritual renewal that could touch your church if it began to trust God in this way. Most of all, you see the need for healing all around you, as well as in your own life, and you believe God wants to use your church to help make people whole.

Now the question becomes how to go about translating dreams into reality. What are some beginning steps? Following are practical how-tos, drawing on the experiences of many churches that have started their own healing ministries.

*Start with yourself, with praying and listening.* We have talked a lot about discernment in this book. In beginning a church healing ministry, discernment is crucial. Listen to the Spirit. Ask yourself: Is this a ministry toward which the Spirit is nudging my church? What specific needs do I see? Am I being called to take the initiative? Does the idea scare me? Excite me?

*Examine your motives for being attracted to healing.* Ask yourself: Am I really only looking for healing for myself ? Or conversely, do I think it is only others who need healing? Am I drawn to the idea because it is a fad or because it seems safer than social action? What needs to happen within me so that I am able to pray wholeheartedly for others?

An invaluable resource for this process of listening to the Spirit is Bible study. Go especially to the healing stories of the Gospels, leisurely recreating the scenes and putting yourself in the presence of Jesus the healer.[1] Expect Jesus to surprise you. Be alert to images, words, and feelings that arise. Prayerfully live with the idea of healing ministry over time and see where—and to whom—the Spirit leads.

*Gather a group of like-minded persons.* From the beginning, be on the lookout for people to share your concern. They may be close friends or people you hardly know. They may be prayer group regulars or people you would not have guessed might be interested. In our experience, almost every community has people who have experienced healing or who feel a gentle nudging toward healing prayer but who have not shared their feelings with others. Part of your job is simply to be watchful for those whom the Spirit puts in your path. Once people learn of your interest, you probably will soon discover kindred souls.

As companions come forth, gather as a group to discern what should be happening in your church. Focus on listening to the Spirit through prayer, silence, Bible study, and discussion. Share your own needs for healing, and pray for each other. Do not hurry the process. Very likely, you will find individuals' energy and sensitivity multiplied in a group setting.

Involve laity and clergy. For laity exploring healing prayer in their churches, it is a good idea neither to run to the pastor, nor to do an end-run around the pastor. On the one hand, healing prayer is a ministry of the whole church. It should not be the sole responsibility of the pastoral staff. Sometimes lay people just assume healing prayer must be initiated by the professionally religious, so they sit back and wait for the pastor to initiate action.

On the other hand, it would be a mistake to go very far in exploring healing prayer without involving the pastoral staff. Clergy attitudes toward the subject of healing vary widely. Sometimes a layperson will say in a workshop, "Why isn't my minister interested in this!?" And it is true that for a variety of reasons many ministers are unacquainted with or are apprehensive about healing in the church. But increasingly, clergy are sensing the potential of ministries of healing and express a desire to work in partnership with their parishioners. Keep in mind that some clergy are just waiting for a glimmer of interest from the laity.

As a general rule, it is good for laity and clergy to cooperate in the exploration early on, keeping in mind the wide variety of styles of pastoral leadership and congregational organization.

*Together, ask what style of healing ministry best suits your church.* By "style of ministry" we mean habits of congregational life as they are shaped by denominational and confessional heritage, patterns of worship, social ethos, demographics, shared memories, and so on. The practices of a rural congregation of Mennonites will probably differ from those of an urban Roman Catholic parish. A small congregation whose average age is sixty will have a different style from a young and growing church of the same denomination. Pay special attention to preferred styles of worship when developing healing ministries. Sacramental, charismatic, and free churches, for example, will prefer types of public healing services noticeably different from each other.

*Together, ask what types of organized healing prayer ministry will best suit your church.* Three typical kinds of healing ministry in a local church setting are (1) public worship, (2) healing prayer groups, and (3) healing teams. (Each of these will be described later in this chapter.) Decisions about structure should involve the whole congregation, but it is good to start thinking about structure at this exploratory stage. The distinctive needs, gifts, and personality of your church will suggest the right kind of prayer for you. Of course, you can expect this to change and evolve over time.

*Share your call to healing ministry with the church leadership.* So far, you and your companions have been listening and imagining possibilities, not making decisions for other people. At some point you need to take your concern to the official structures of the church. It is important that a healing ministry be understood and supported by the whole church. Too long relegated to the margins, healing prayer needs to be brought into the center of the church's life and given institutional credibility.

Two things should happen almost simultaneously in this process: consultation and study. Communicate your vision of a healing community to those responsible for worship, spiritual life, and social concerns in your church. Invite leaders into an exploration of the possibilities for your church, beginning with their own need for healing. Tell your own stories. Remember that it is not first a matter of another new program but of responding to a call.

While personal testimony is vital, it is also important for people to define terms, deal with questions and doubts, examine various styles, and, most important, experience for themselves God's healing presence and love. Invite church leaders and decision makers to gather for short courses that include Bible study of Jesus' healings, reading and discussing books on the subject, and gentle experiences of healing prayer.[2]

What organizational form your church's healing ministry should take depends on many variables. Initiative may reside in the pastoral staff, in a standing committee, or in a newly formed structure. You may be at the center of it, or you may need to entrust your vision to others. What is important is that the church hears Jesus' invitation and begins to stretch out its hands in ways that take root and grow in the lives of people.

*Be a healer in your community.* Despite our best efforts and hopes, sometimes things do not work out the way we want. Others do not share our vision of healing in the church, or the time is not right, and so on. Whether or not your church develops a structured healing ministry, you can still respond to your call by being a channel of healing among your friends, your family, and in the community.

*Expect the Holy Spirit to show you the way.* The last word in our discussion of practical steps is an encouraging one. If it is true that God is calling churches to a renewal of healing in our time, then we can trust that God will go before us when we step out in obedience. "Stepping out" needs to be done with wisdom and good sense. One minister, without warning, impulsively announced during a Sunday worship service that anyone wishing to receive healing prayers and anointing could remain after the service. Surprisingly, most of the congregation stayed! Going about it that way is surely imprudent, but the story does suggest that we should not timidly underestimate people's readiness to venture forth in healing. Nor should we underestimate the Spirit's influence in preparing the way.

## Three Models of Congregational Healing Ministry

What specific forms might healing ministries take in a local congregation? We briefly describe three familiar models. (See the resources in the bibliography for further information.)

### Public Worship

In the context of regular services of worship, a general prayer for healing can be offered, perhaps as part of the general prayers of intercession. Or, with preparation, a prayer can name particular persons' needs, which have been solicited beforehand. This practice requires tact and good judgment but can deepen trust and support within the congregation. It can also be a good first step toward deeper involvement in healing ministry.

Prayers for healing can play a more prominent part in the service. A common pattern is for worshipers to come to the altar or communion rail near the end of the service where the minister(s) lays on hands and/or anoints and offers a prayer for healing. The prayer can be either the same brief prayer said for each person or an extemporaneous prayer tailored to the request of each individual who comes forward. Another pattern is for trained healing teams of two or three people to be stationed at the altar or about the sanctuary to receive those who wish to come for prayers at a designated time, for example, immediately after receiving Communion or immediately after the benediction.

A number of denominations include orders for public services of healing in their books of worship.3 These services have the advantage of making healing the central theme of an entire service of worship and are usually offered on a weekly or monthly basis or on special occasions.

The most important service of healing in the church is the Sacrament of Holy Communion. The service can readily be adapted to include prayers for healing and even laying on of hands and anointing. Even without these, many find the Eucharist a time when they experience the healing presence of Christ in a special way. One pastor holds an eight o'clock Eucharist with healing prayers every Sunday morning before the regular eleven o'clock service. He says the early service consistently nourishes him.

*Building acts of healing into a church's public worship communicates that healing has been placed at the center of the church's ministry.* Through its central acts of worship the church shows itself to be a healing community.

## Healing Prayer Groups (Praying for Others)

Most congregations have prayer groups of various sorts, but here we think particularly of groups whose specific and intentional focus is praying for healing. Groups may meet regularly—perhaps once every week or two—for at least an hour. The ideal size is six to eight people. They pray not only for those whose needs are made known to them, but also for each other. They also pray for the healing of institutions as well as for individuals. Healing prayer groups minister deeply to their own congregations as the group prays for the church's healing persistently and over time.

## Healing Teams (Praying with Others)

Healing teams are specially trained to engage in a more direct and intense form of healing ministry. Healing teams are trained not only to pray for others but to pray with people as well. Picture a prayer team of two to four people gathered about a person who has requested their prayers. They may pray with a person only once or, more likely, many times over a longer period. Their own spiritual preparation, training, and motivation equip them to move deeply into the needs for healing brought to them. Team members need to be spiritually mature and emotionally healthy, with a clear sense of call to this ministry.

A team's training begins with praying for each other and experiencing God's healing in themselves. They learn to feel comfortable with deeply felt emotion and with praying both aloud and in silence. They learn to listen to those who come for prayer and to the Spirit's direction on how to pray for each one. They listen too for the difference between the Spirit and their own inner "static."

Along the way, the healing team continues to discern prayerfully what it is doing, and it stays open to changing its structures or style.

A wise healing prayer team focuses not upon how many people ask for prayers, or on how many are healed, or even upon what it wants for a particular person. The focus stays on what God desires to do.

Personal issues inevitably arise within prayer teams, who are after all wounded healers. Praying for others will surely open up areas of pain in team members. For this reason, some teams periodically work with a psychotherapist, pastoral counselor, or spiritual director who can help them process their experience.

## A Final Word: "I Send You Forth to Heal"

Our exploration began with Jesus' words to the man with a withered hand, "Stretch out your hand!" In those words we heard Jesus inviting not just one wounded person but all his followers to stretch out their hands toward him and toward others. In the pages that followed we have considered many stories of healing and what healing means; dealt with questions about the theory and practice of healing; looked at praying for the healing of self, others, and institutions; and portrayed the church as the unique community where Christian healing happens. Through all this we have been preparing to respond to Jesus' invitation.

As our exploration concludes, we turn to another scene from Jesus' ministry. This time we encounter Jesus teaching, preaching, and healing in Galilee:

> Then Jesus went about all the cities and villages, teaching in their synagogues, and proclaiming the good news of the kingdom, and curing every disease and every sickness. When he saw the crowds, he had compassion for them, because they were harassed and helpless, like

sheep without a shepherd. Then he said to his disciples, "The harvest is plentiful, but the laborers are few; therefore ask the Lord of the harvest to send out laborers into his harvest" (Matt. 9:35-38).

We are struck by the way Jesus' most characteristic acts—teaching, preaching, and healing—are closely linked. We see Jesus' compassion for the crowds. We sense his urgency for the harvest. Perhaps we can see ourselves both as members of the helpless crowd and as potential laborers for the harvest. Then the scene changes:

> Then Jesus summoned his twelve disciples and gave them authority over unclean spirits, to cast them out, and to cure every disease and every sickness.... These twelve Jesus sent out with the following instructions: "... As you go, proclaim the good news, 'The kingdom of heaven has come near.' Cure the sick, raise the dead, cleanse the lepers, cast out demons. You received without payment; give without payment" (Matt. 10:1, 5a, 7-8).

Again, in the clearest terms Jesus joins the act of healing to the task of preaching God's reign. He commissions the twelve to carry on his own ministry, giving them the power to heal and authority over evil. In the boldest possible way, he sends them forth to heal.

Picture the twelve listening incredulously to Jesus' commission, dumbfounded at the gift and challenge bestowed on them. "Who are we to receive such a mission?" they ask. "Where will we get the strength?" Imagine the circle of the twelve parting, opening to include other disciples with other names—old and young, women and men—from every people under the sun. See the circle widen even more to include your life's companions, teachers, and role models—your helpers and healers. See at last the circle widen to make a place for you among the disciples. Hear Jesus say simply and firmly to you, "I send you forth to heal!"

As you imagine that scene, what other images, associations, and thoughts arise? What emotions are stirred? Welcome whatever comes to you, alert to the next steps and new directions for your journey in healing.

Bob remembers: Once I was leading a clergy workshop through this guided imagery exercise. With the other participants I sat in silence hearing Jesus say to me, "Bob, I send you forth to heal." "What does that mean for me?" I thought. "I'm a teacher, not a pastor. I don't have a 'gift' of healing. Where is Jesus sending me?" I then became aware of the others in the room, ministers earnestly exploring what healing prayer meant for them. The realization came to me: Jesus is calling me to be a healer by offering hospitality to healers! I saw myself in my own place of vocation helping to prepare the ground and tend the growth of the church's healing ministry, through these ministers and other clergy and laity to follow. That insight continues to form part of my call.

Though the shape of our calls will vary according to our particular gifts and the world's needs, Jesus speaks these words to each of his followers, sending forth every Christian to be a healer. Pause to listen as Jesus says, in a way you will be able to hear, "I send you forth to heal."

# NOTES

## Chapter One

1. It was not possible to follow up with the man to determine the long-term effects of the prayer.
2. Morton Kelsey has compiled a brief history of healing from the Bible to the present in *Healing and Christianity: A Classic Study,* 3rd ed. (Minneapolis, MN: Augsburg Press, 1995), 83–201.
3. *Against Celsus* 1.46,67; quoted in Kelsey, *Healing and Christianity,* 120.
4. For a fascinating study of healing and health in Eastern Orthodoxy, see Stanley S. Harakas, *Health and Medicine in the Eastern Orthodox Tradition* (New York: Crossroad Publishing, 1991).
5. Kelsey, *Healing and Christianity,* 158.
6. Ibid., 145ff.
7. *Summa Theologica* III.44.3; Ad. 1 and 3, quoted in ibid., 169.
8. *Calvin: Institutes of the Christian Religion* IV.19.18; ed. John T. McNeill and trans. Ford Lewis Battles, vol. XXI, 1467, of Library of Christian Classics. ed. John Baille, John T. McNeill, and Hanry P. Van Dusen (Philadelphia, PA: Westminster Press, 1960).
9. Quoted in Kelsey, *Healing and Christianity,* 183.
10. Ibid., 182–85.

## Chapter Two

1. Larry Dossey, M.D., *Healing Words: The Power of Prayer and the Practice of*

*Medicine* (San Francisco: HarperSanFrancisco, 1995), has collected scores of scientific studies and clinical histories in order to demonstrate the connection between prayer, healing, and medicine. See also Kenneth R. Pelletier, *Mind as Healer, Mind as Slayer* (New York: Dell Publishing, 1977); O. Carl Simonton, Matthews-Simonton, and Creighton, *Getting Well Again* (New York: Bantam Books, 1982); Bernie S. Siegel, M.D., *Love, Medicine, and Miracles* (New York: HarperCollins, 1986).

2. See, for example, Fritjof Capra, *The Tao of Physics* (Berkeley, CA: Shambhala Publications, 1971); Gary Zukav, *The Dancing Wu Li Masters* (New York: Bantam Books, 1984).

3. For a Process Theology interpretation of miraculous healing, see Barry L. Whitney, *Evil and the Process God* (New York and Toronto: Edwin Mellen Press, 1985), 124–131. For a Protestant Evangelical theological defense of miracles see Colin Brown, *Miracles and the Critical Mind* (Grand Rapids, MI:Wm.B. Eerdmans Publishing, 1984). See especially the biblically radical perspective of Walter Wink, *Engaging the Powers* (Minneapolis, MN: Ausburg Fortress Publishers, 1992), 303.

4. See also Job 5:18. Death and illness are often represented as punishment for disobedience and sin: Genesis 20; Numbers 12; Deuteronomy 28:27-35; Psalms 32:3-4; 38:1-12; 41:4; 107:17-22.

5. Jesus' Gethsemane prayer is a stumbling block to some who take it to mean they should not pray for healing. But see Francis S. MacNutt, *The Power to Heal* (Notre Dame, IN: Ave Maria Press, 1977), 134ff.

6. In recent years the lines have blurred between fundamentalist, evangelical, and charismatic Christians on the question of healing. See James Barr, *Fundamentalism* (Philadelphia, PA: Westminster Press, 1977), 207.

7. See Robert McAfee Brown, *Spirituality and Liberation* (Philadelphia, PA: Westminster Press, 1988).

8. We address this issue at length in chapter 5.

9. See the helpful discussion of this in Francis MacNutt, *Healing* (Altamonte Springs, FL: Creation House, 1988), 119–25.

10. Space does not permit a full treatment of these texts. For a thorough, scholarly study of the healing stories of the Gospels, see John P. Meier,

*A Marginal Jew: Rethinking the Historical Jesus*, vol. 2, *Mentor, Message, and Miracles* (New York: Doubleday, 1994), 509–873.

11. On Jesus' "forceful and imaginative speech," see Robert C. Tannehill, *The Sword of His Mouth* (Philadelphia, PA: Fortress Press, 1975).

12. Think of the figures of Job (prior to Job 42:7), Jeremiah (Jer. 15:15-21), and Paul (2 Cor. 12:7-10).

13. We discuss the importance of spiritual discernment in chapters 3–5.

14. For other approaches to the question of why healing does not happen, see MacNutt, *Healing*, 255–68; and James K. Wagner, *Blessed to Be a Blessing* (Nashville, TN: The Upper Room, 1980), 64–76.

15. This is the subject of chapter 6.

## *Chapter Three*

1. See Matthew Linn, Sheila Fabricant, and Dennis Linn, *Healing the Eight Stages of Life* (Mahwah, NJ: Paulist Press, 1988).

2. An accessible modern edition is by George E. Ganss, SJ, *The Spiritual Exercises of Saint Ignatius* (Chicago: Loyola University Press, 1992).

3. Scripture, tradition, experience, and reason are the four formative factors of theology named in *The Book of Discipline of The United Methodist Church* (Nashville, TN: Abingdon Press, 1988), 81–86. See also John Macquarrie, *Principles of Christian Theology*, 2nd ed. (New York: Scribner's, 1977), 4–18.

4. See Abraham Schmitt, *Before I Wake* (Nashville, TN: Abingdon Press, 1984).

5. See Jerome M. Neufelder and Mary C. Coelho, eds., *Writings on Spiritual Direction* (New York: Seabury Press, 1982), 117–39.

6. Fritz Perls, the founder of Gestalt therapy, often told his students, "the hardest thing in the world to give up is your suffering."

7. Siegel, *Love, Medicine, and Miracles*, 65–99; also O. Carl Simonton, Stephanie Matthews-Simonton, and James L. Creighton, *Getting Well Again*, 107–13.

8. Francis MacNutt, *The Power to Heal*, 39–55.

9. For further exploration of faith imagination, also called "healing of memories" or "inner healing," see Matthew Linn, Dennis Linn, and Sheila Fabricant, *Prayer Course for Healing Life's Hurts* (New York: Paulist Press, 1983); Francis S. MacNutt, *Healing*, 181–97; Theodore Elliott Dobson, *Inner Healing* (New York: Paulist Press, 1979).

10. See for example Matthew 12:22-32; Mark 1:21-28; 9:14-29; Romans 8:35-39; Galatians 4:8-9; Ephesians 6:10-12; Colossians 1:11-20.

11. See Francis MacNutt, *Deliverance from Evil Spirits* (Grand Rapids, MI: Chosen Books, 1995); Matthew Linn and Dennis Linn, *Deliverance Prayer* (New York: Paulist Press, 1981); Don Basham, *Deliver Us from Evil* (Lincoln, VA: Chosen Books, 1972); Kenneth McAll, *Healing the Family Tree* (London: Sheldon Press, 1982).

## Chapter Four

1. See Dennis Linn, Matthew Linn, and Sheila Fabricant, *Praying with Another for Healing* (New York: Paulist Press, 1984).

2. See the classic by Henri J. M. Nouwen, *The Wounded Healer* (Garden City, NY: Image Books, 1972).

3. Healing teams are discussed in chapter 6.

4. For an accessible discussion of this kind of listening, see Thomas Gordon, "How to Listen So Kids Will Talk to You: The Language of Acceptance," chap. 3 in P.E.T. (New York: NAL Dutton, 1975).

## Chapter Five

1. Elizabeth O'Connor, *Journey Inward, Journey Outward* (San Francisco: HarperSanFrancisco, 1975).

2. Quoted in Kenneth L. Bakken, *The Call to Wholeness: Health as a Spiritual Journey* (New York: Crossroad Publishing, 1985), 8.

3. "[In the Old Testament], the emphasis tends to be relational: peace exists between people or between people and God. The idea of peace as individual spiritual peace with God or internal peace of mind is not an Old Testament notion," s.v., "Peace," *The HarperCollins Bible Dictionary*, ed. Paul J. Achtemeier (New York: HarperCollins, 1985, 1996), 823.

4. Commenting on Exodus 15:26, Walter Brueggemann declares the intention of God "is to restore persons, communities, and ultimately the whole of creation to their rightful status of health, as creatures loved by and responsive to the purposes of the creator," in "The Book of Exodus," *The New Interpreter's Bible* 1 (Nashville, TN: Abingdon Press, 1994), 809.

5. John P. Meier, *A Marginal Jew*, vol. 2 (New York: Doubleday, 1994), 837.

6. For a political interpretation of Mark 5:1-20, see Ched Myers, *Binding the Strong Man: A Political Reading of Mark's Story of Jesus* (Maryknoll, NY: Orbis Books, 1988), 190–94.

7. Walter Wink calls Jesus' cleansing of the Temple "the paradigmatic collective exorcism in the New Testament," in *Unmasking the Powers: The Invisible Forces That Determine Human Existence* (Philadelphia, Pa.: Fortress Press, 1986), 65. See the bibliography for full reference to Wink's trilogy on the Powers, a fundamental resource for any study of confronting social evil.

8. We draw upon his essay, "Social Exorcism," in *Journey Toward Justice: Commemorating the 80th Anniversary of the Social Creed of the People Called Methodists*, Jan Kindwoman and Ron Ozier eds. (Staten Island, NY: The Methodist Federation for Social Action, 1988), 116–33. George D. McClain has further developed his work of combining spirituality and social action in his book, *Claiming All Things For God: Prayer, Discernment, and Ritual for Social Change* (Nashville, TN: Abingdon Press, 1998).

9. McClain, *Claiming All Things*, 120–21.

10. McClain, "Social Exorcism," 116.

11. Ibid., 119.

12. Ibid., 123.

13. Ibid., 125.

14. McClain, *Claiming All Things*, 123.

15. McClain, "Social Exorcism," 129.

16. Ibid., 132. The reference is to Walter Brueggemann, *Hopeful Imagination: Prophetic Voices in Exile* (Philadelphia, PA: Fortress Press, 1986), 17f. See also *Claiming All Things*, chap. 3, "The Silent Tyranny of the Modern Worldview."

17. This was clearly recognized by South African Christians in the anti-apartheid struggle. See, for example, the sermon that Dr. Allan A. Boesak preached on the tenth anniversary of the Soweto uprising: "I Have Seen Satan Fall," in *If This Is Treason, I Am Guilty* (Grand Rapids, MI: Eerdmans Wm B., Trenton, NJ: African World Press, 1987), 125–34.

18. Wink, *Unmasking the Powers*, 64f.

19. This service was adapted by Tilda Norberg from one devised by George D. McClain and is used by permission.

## *Chapter Six*

1. For a method of placing yourself imaginatively in the scenes of the Bible, see William A. Barry, SJ, *Who Do You Say That I Am?* (Notre Dame, IN: Ave Maria Press, 1996). For readable brief studies of the healing stories of the Gospels, consult the following commentaries: Lamar Williamson, Jr. *Mark*, Interpretation (Atlanta: John Knox Press, 1983); Douglas R. A. Hare, *Matthew*, Interpretation (Louisville, KY: John Knox Press, 1993); Robert C. Tannehill, *Luke*, Abingdon New Testament Commentaries (Nashville, TN: Abingdon Press, 1996); Luke Timothy Johnson, *Luke*, Sacra Pagina Series (Collegeville, MN: Liturgical Press, 1991); Gerard S. Sloyan, *John*, Interpretation (Atlanta: John Knox Press, 1988).

2. The book in hand, with its accompanying Leader's Guide, is designed for just this purpose, as is James K. Wagner, *An Adventure in Healing and Wholeness: The Healing Ministry of Christ in the Church Today* (Nashville, TN:

The Upper Room, 1993). See the bibliography for other resources, and the preceding note for Bible study resources.

3. See, for example, the following denominational worship resources: *Book of Worship: Church of the Brethren* (Elgin, IL: Brethren Press, 1964), "The Anointing Service," 226–30; The Book of Common Prayer (Episcopal) (New York: Oxford University Press, 1979), "Ministration to the Sick," 453–61; *Occasional Services: A Companion to the Lutheran Book of Worship* (Minneapolis, MN: Augsburg Publishing House, 1982); *Book of Worship: United Church of Christ* (New York: United Church of Christ Office for Church Life and Leadership, 1986), "Services of Reconciliation and Healing," 268–320; *The United Methodist Book of Worship* (Nashville, TN: United Methodist Publishing House, 1992), "Healing Services and Prayers" 613–29; *Services for Occasions of Pastoral Care* (Louisville, KY: Westminster/John Knox Press, 1990). For use in the Presbyterian Church (U.S.A.) and the Cumberland Presbyterian Church.

# SELECTED BIBLIOGRAPHY

Bakken, Kenneth L., M.D. *The Call to Wholeness: Health as a Spiritual Journey.* New York: Crossroad Publishing, 1985. A Christian healer and physician stresses the connections of body, mind, and spirit.

Clinebell, Howard, Ph.D. *Anchoring Your Well Being: Christian Wholeness in a Fractured World.* Nashville, TN: Upper Room Books, 1997. Also *Anchoring Your Well Being: A Guide for Congregational Leaders.* Nashville, TN: Upper Room Books, 1997.

Dobson, Theodore E. *Inner Healing: God's Great Assurance.* New York: Paulist Press, 1978. Emphasizes faith imagination, and the healer's discernment.

Dossey, Larry, M.D. *Healing Words: The Power of Prayer and the Practice of Medicine.* San Francisco: HarperSanFrancisco, 1993.

Guenther, Margaret. *Holy Listening: The Art of Spiritual Direction.* Boston, MA: Cowley Publications, 1992. Using metaphors of hospitality and midwifery, Guenther beautifully illumines the holy process of listening for God's invitation together.

Kelsey, Morton. *Healing and Christianity: A Classic Study.* Third ed. Minneapolis, MN: Augsburg Fortress, 1995. Traces the history of Christian healing from its biblical roots to today's holistic perspective.

Linn, Dennis, and Matthew Linn. *Healing Life's Hurts: Healing Memories Through the Five Stages of Forgiveness.* New York: Paulist Press, 1978. Based on Dr. Elisabeth Kuebler-Ross's five stages of dying.

_____. *Healing of Memories: Prayers and Confession—Steps to Inner Healing.* New York: Paulist Press, 1974. A how-to book for personal or group study.

Linn, Dennis; Sheila Fabricant; and Matthew Linn. *Praying with Another for Healing*. New York: Paulist Press, 1984. A good introductory workbook.

McClain, George D. *Claiming All Things for God: Prayer, Discernment, and Ritual for Social Change*. Nashville, TN: Abingdon Press, 1998.

MacNutt, Francis. *Healing*. Rev. ed. Altamonte Springs, FL: Creation House, 1988. Still the basic book on healing, rich in practical and theological insight. The revised edition is addressed to an ecumenical audience.

_____. *The Power to Heal*. Notre Dame, IN: Ave Maria Press, 1977. A valuable supplement to *Healing*.

_____. *Deliverance from Evil Spirits: A Practical Manual*. Grand Rapids, MI: Chosen Books, 1995. Offers balanced and sane pastoral guidance, psychological insight, and practical advice for ministers of healing.

Meier, John P. *A Marginal Jew: Rethinking the Historical Jesus*. vol. 2: *Mentor, Message, and Miracles*. New York: Doubleday, 1994. Exhaustive study of Jesus' healings by a historian of early Christianity.

Norberg, Tilda and Joyce Thomas, illus. *Threadbear: A Story of Christian Healing for Adult Survivors of Sexual Abuse*. Staten Island, NY: Penn House Press, 1997. (To order call 718-273-4941.) Chronicles steps in the healing process and provides over forty drawings that serve as healing "icons" for survivors in recovery.

Schmitt, Abraham. *Before I Wake: Listening to God in Your Dreams*. Nashville, TN: Abingdon Press, 1984. A good beginning book on personal dream work by a psychologist.

Siegel, Bernie S., M.D. *Love, Medicine, and Miracles: Lessons Learned about Self-Healing from a Surgeon's Experience with Exceptional Patients*. New York: HarperCollins, 1990. This physician's work with "exceptional patients" offers evidence for the power of the mind to heal the body.

Wink, Walter. *Naming the Powers: The Language of Power in the New Testament*. Minneapolis, MN: Augsburg Fortress, 1984.

_____. *Unmasking the Powers: The Invisible Forces that Determine Human Existence*. Minneapolis, MN: Augsburg Fortress, 1986.

_____. *Engaging the Powers: Discernment and Resistance in a World of Domination*. Minneapolis, MN: Augsburg Fortress, 1992. Three works of fundamental importance on the calling of Christians to encounter the spiritual realities of the world. (Also published in one volume as *The Powers That Be: Theology for a New Millen[n]nium.* New York: Doubleday, 1998.)

CPSIA information can be obtained
at www.ICGtesting.com
Printed in the USA
FFHW021407111118
49298300-53531FF

9 780835 808729